A Perfect Life

A Plain Account of Christian Perfection

A Perfect Life

A Plain Account of Christian Perfection

By John Wesley

Updated and Paraphrased by Bo Cassell

ANCIENT FAITH SERIES

Barefoot Ministries®
Kansas City, Missouri

Copyright 2005
by Barefoot Ministries®

ISBN 083-415-0077

Printed in the
United States of America

Editor: Stephanie McNelly
Cover Design: Kevin Williamson

Library of Congress Cataloging-in-Publication Data

Wesley, John, 1703-1791.
  A perfect life : the plain account of Christian perfection / by John Wesley.—
Updated and paraphrased / by Bo Cassell.
     p. cm. — (Ancient faith series)
  Rev. ed. of: A plain account of Christian perfection. 1968.
  ISBN 0-8341-5007-7
  1. Perfection—Religious aspects—Christianity. 2. Youth—Religious life. I. Cassell, Bo. II. Wesley, John, 1703-1791. Plain account of Christian perfection. III. Title. IV. Series.

  BT766.W52 2005
  234—dc22

2004026956

10   9   8   7   6   5   4   3   2   1

CONTENTS

For Jesus, my Lord, and Tish, my wife—
both of whom see all my imperfection and love me anyway.

PREFACE

In *A Perfect Life*, Bo Cassell has updated and paraphrased John Wesley's classic *A Plain Account of Christian Perfection*, in which Wesley comprehensively explains his views on Christian perfection and holiness in a unique format—sometimes he writes journal entries, at other times it is like reading a frequently asked question sheet on the topic.

On the following pages you will encounter excerpts from Wesley's sermons and writings, lines from hymns that he and his brother Charles wrote, and various question and answer sessions. No matter what format he uses, however, Wesley plainly explains how to live a holy and perfect life.

So no matter where you are on your Christian walk—whether you are a brand-new Christian or you have been one for many years—sit back and let God talk to you about living the perfect life through the thoughts of John Wesley.

A Note About This Book and the Series

This book is part of a series called "The Ancient Faith Series." It is our hope to take some of the thoughts and writings from those who have gone before us, and breathe new life into their words of wisdom which have stood the test of time. By "remixing" the outdated language, we can bring the heart and intention of some of the great lessons of the faith into the present.

With this work by John Wesley, we tried to stay as faithful to the meaning and intention of the original writer as possible. At times, we have quoted him word for word, and at other times summarized a few sentences with just one, or elaborated and added a phrase or two in order to explain clearly the topic at hand. We cut some parts that were redundant or specific to the time in which Wesley lived. Throughout the book we have done whatever we could to bring out the meaning of the writer, but place it in modern language. Our intention has been to take the ancient work and make it relevant.

Wesley's work possesses some interesting challenges—he was writing in his day to answer certain questions in the midst of a great work of God that faced misunderstandings and opposition. There are details about people and responses to questions that were raised by all that God was doing in their midst.

In this sense, this book raises a particular challenge—it occurred to us that Wesley is answering questions that no one is asking today. The closer we tried to stay to the original work, the more difficult it became to stay relevant to the present. Much of what this book does is to try to answer questions surrounding a revival through which people were experiencing holiness. For us today, who did not see all of this happening around us, it is strange to read questions and answers pulled from the context of the fire, passion, and challenges of living in the midst of a great work of God.

That very fact brings up another problem—a good one. In this book you will encounter answers to questions that are not being asked today. Which brings us to other questions: Has God ever stopped asking His people to walk in holiness with Him? If not, then why aren't we asking these questions? Why aren't more people pursuing a perfect life with all the passion that they have within them? And this key question—do you want to be holy?

It is our hope that this book at the very least, will begin to raise the question of a perfect life of holiness for the present generation, and for generations to come. It is our hope that youth and adults alike will begin to talk about and seek to love and live for God in the way described within these pages, and these ancient truths will rekindle present renewal.

(The author would like to acknowledge that one of Wesley's statements was perfectly paraphrased by Dana Walling shortly before his death in the year 2000, and has been included here. Those who knew him will know it when they read it—though it is only one sentence in this work. It is worth mentioning in part because Dana Walling represents one of those people who lived in such a way that gives us hope that we can live a perfect life here on earth. He was one of those Wesley spoke about—someone we could point to and say, "the perfect life is real.")

1 THE PURPOSE OF THIS BOOK

What follows is my attempt to tell the simple and under-standable story of the steps involved in living a holy and godly life—a "Perfect Life," or as some call it, the life of "Christian Perfection." These steps were presented to me and I have walked them over the last few years, embracing them as a straight road to walk. I wanted to tell all of you who are seri-ous about not wasting your life—those who want to know all the truth—how it really is in Jesus. (Who else would want to devote themselves to a life lived completely for God?) To you, I am here to tell nakedly and plainly the truth as it really is—here is what I think about living a perfect life . . .

2 BEING COMPLETELY DEDICATED

At the age of 23, I came across a book called the *Rule and Exercises of Holy Living and Dying*. When I read it, it was like I was kicked in the gut. One part in particular jumped out at me—the part about having pure intentions. Right then and there, I resolved to dedicate all my life to God. I determined to give Him all my thoughts, words, and actions; I became thor-oughly convinced that there is no middle ground—there is no room for being wishy-washy. Every part of my life—every part—not just some of my life, but *all of my life* must be a sacrifice to God.

I realized in that moment that my life was either a sacrifice to God or to myself. And if I was hoarding my life for myself, I was in effect taking it away from God and offering it to the devil. I know that may sound harsh, but listen: If you are really serious about not wasting your life, think about this—if you have not to-tally given your life back to God and surrendered to His perfect plans, are you not in fact squandering your life away on your-self? And if you are squandering your life away on yourself, aren't you then more useful to the devil than to God?

3 A Simple, Singular Intention

The next year, I ran across a book written by a man named Kempis that talked about a new pattern for Christian living. The book was like a spotlight on my soul, and it helped me understand what it means to have an "inner religion." There is an outer religion of our actions—going to church and doing good things—but there is also an inner religion, a religion of the heart, where we live out what we believe in ways that no one can see. I realized when reading this book that even if I gave God my whole life (all my actions) it wouldn't do me any good unless I gave Him my inner life as well. (Is it really possible to separate the two, to divorce your inner life from your outer life?) I realized that only giving God my outer life (what I do) was a charade—it was me putting on a front—if I did not in fact also give Him my will, my desires, and my thoughts—the religion of the deepest parts of my heart.

You've heard of having good intentions, right? I saw the benefit of having a singular intention—one aim in my life—a pure love for God and God alone. My eyes were opened to the freedom of having one motivation behind all my words and all my actions—just one desire ruling over the character of my life. The thought of that freedom made my soul feel light; it was as if I had the freedom of wings and could fly straight toward God. The thought of not having that freedom made my soul heavy; it was like I was tired at the bottom of a mountain, too heavy and burdened to climb up to be with God on the heights.

4 No "Half Christians"

A year or two after reading Kempis's book, a friend loaned me two books written by William Law—*Christian Perfection* and *A Serious Call to the Devout and Holy Life.* The Christian life described in those books convinced me, more than ever, of the absolute impossibility of being a half Christian. I knew that I could not live the real thing without the grace of God in my life—His grace was absolutely necessary—without it I would never make it. I determined, through God's grace, to be wholly devoted to Him, to give Him all my soul, body, and very being. This *was* a serious call—it was either all in or all out, right now.

How could any realistic person say that this was going too far—that I was becoming some kind of fanatic or freak? If you really take the time to think about it, what do we owe God? Everything! How could we give anything less than our all, our everything, to Him who has given himself for us? How could we give Him anything less than ourselves, all we have, and all we are?

5 BECOMING LIKE CHRIST

About three years later, I began to change the way I studied the Bible—I began to look at the Bible as the one and only standard of truth in a deceptive, "spin-filled" world. The Bible became the standard I used to measure true and pure religion. As I studied this way, it became clearer and clearer to me that it was absolutely necessary to have the mind of Christ and to walk in the way that Christ walked. I began to realize that it was vitally important to have not just a part of the mind of Christ, but to have *all* of the mind of Christ—His mind should fill my head and thoughts. It was equally important to walk as Christ walked, not in some or most ways, but in all ways.

As the Bible brought light to my thoughts, I began to see that Christianity could only be a pure religion if we follow Christ in every way possible. In other words, real Christianity is when our whole life—inner and outer—conforms completely to the life of Christ, our Master. When I came to this realization, I was scared to death! I was frightened that I would be tempted to make Christianity something less than this—I was afraid of lowering this standard to my own opinion or to the opinion of others. I was afraid that I would agree with someone who would say "You don't have to follow Christ in every area of your life, only following some will be enough." It scared me to think about becoming the kind of Christian who would live a life that did not completely conform to the life of Jesus Christ and the example He gave us.

6 THE SIGN OF A DEVOTED HEART

It was New Year's Day when I had the opportunity to speak at a university on the topic, "the sacrifice of the heart." I gave an account of my understanding of what it means to have a covenant with God. I said, "When the Bible talks about holiness, it is talking about having a soul whose habits are always inclined to live God's way. To create that habitual life, God must cleanse your heart from sin—clean out the habits of rebellion, disbelief, and disobedience to Him. God will flush away all the filth from your body and spirit and replace your life's filth with virtues—the character qualities of Jesus Christ. Through this cleansing God makes your mind new again and empowers you to 'be perfect . . . as your heavenly Father is perfect' (Matthew 5:48).

"Love is all, it accomplishes everything God intended when He set down rules for us to live by. Love is the end of all God wants for us; it is the first and best part of a perfect life. Love is everything God wishes for us rolled up into one. Love captures all the Bible is talking about when it says, 'Whatever is true, . . . whatever is pure, . . . if anything is excellent or praiseworthy—think about such things' (Philippians 4:8). In love there is perfection, beauty, and happiness. God's kingly decree for heaven and earth is this: Love the King of All, your God, with all your heart, with all your soul, with all your mind, and with all your strength (Deuteronomy 6:5)—love Him with all that makes you who you are. Loving God should be your ultimate goal—the one perfect and good thing you pursue with all your might. You should want one thing for its own sake, that you would be surrounded by God's love and completely able to love Him in return. If you could give your soul one thing to be happy about, let it be this: to be united with the 'Maker of Souls,' to live together with the Father and the Son, to be joined at the hip with God as if the two of you shared one Spirit.

"There is only one real plan and path to follow from now until the end—to utterly enjoy God in the now and in the Forever that will come after. You can love other things, and love people too, but do it in this way: only love the creation in a way that leads to the Creator. In your daily walk, let that be the ending point of your journey. Let every other desire, every thought, every word, and every action come in second place to your love for God."

My last words to them were, "Following God's perfect law can be summed up like this: dedicate your heart to God permanently—like a sacrifice on an altar. Aim to give your spirit back to God who gave it to you in the first place. Point your heart and will in His direction and let every other desire follow in tow. God doesn't want a bunch of dead-end sacrificial responses; He wants only one thing, and that is for you to offer your whole life as a living sacrifice. So continually offer God your heart and life. Be on fire for Him until everything else is burned away and only your pure love for Him remains. Don't let anything in creation share God's place. He has told us that He is a jealous God, and He won't share His place in your life with anything else. God the King will not cut His throne in half and let someone else sit next to Him as coruler. He reigns over all, and He has no rival. So don't allow any puny plan or gainful lust into His throne room. Only God-centered plans and dreams have a place there. We can only have the mind of Christ in us when every pursuit of our hearts, every word of our mouths, and every work of our hands seeks nothing but those things that connect us to God. The only chance we have at having the same mind as Christ is when we put all these things behind our desire to please God. When we can say like Christ, 'I have come . . . not to do my will but to do the will of him who sent me' (John 6:38), then we have the mind of Christ. It is like the Bible says, whatever 'you eat or drink or whatever you do, do it all for the glory of God'" (1 Corinthians 10:31).

This speech summarized the view of religion I had at that time. Even then I did not hesitate to call this way of living "a perfect life." I believe the same things today; I haven't flip-flopped or changed any part of it. I keep wondering, how can anyone who believes the Bible argue against the ideas that Christ can give us a perfect life and the ability to follow Him completely? These ideas are built on Scripture. You can't deny this life I have described without denying the content of the Bible. You can't put it aside without surgically removing passages of the Bible from your life. If you say, "this doesn't apply to me," then you are saying that God's intention for your life doesn't apply to you.

7 "ONLY THE PURE LOVE OF GOD"

My brother and I held on to this headlong passionate pursuit of God (along with others who were ridiculed for it and called "Methodizers" for the intentional method we took to make sure God was first in our lives). We viewed it as the most important thing in our lives, and it stayed with us as we grew older, into our middle years and beyond. The intensity did not die; in fact, as time went on I felt called into missionary service and left my home in England to serve as a missionary across the Atlantic in Georgia. There in Savannah, I captured the feeling of the fire within me in a few lines of poetry:

> In this world, is there anything
> That wrestles God to share my heart?
> Please tear it out, my only King
> You are the Lord of every part.

Three years later, I returned to England, and the fire within me had the same brightness as when I left:

> God grant that nothing in my soul
> Remains, but Your pure love alone!
> And may Your love possess me whole,
> My joy, my treasure, and my crown.
> Rival fires quench and remove,
> 'Till all I think and do is LOVE!

No one who read those words ever told me they thought it was a bad way of thinking, or that I lacked passion for God. My words were the language of awakening, of being alive.

8 FULL ASSURANCE OF FAITH

In the summer of the next year, I had a talk with an old friend. He told me of his own experience of waking up to a new understanding of faith in God. I asked him to give me an account of his experience in writing, defining what he meant when he said he had a "full assurance of faith." Here is what he wrote:

> Rest in the blood of Christ;
> Confidently trust in God,
> Convinced that God's grace is free,
> Have the highest ease of soul and peace of mind,
> Knowing that you have been delivered from all desires of the flesh,
> To the point that even the deepest inner sin of the heart has stopped.

This was the first time that I had ever heard another living person talk about the very same thing that God's Word had been speaking to me about, and I had been praying for (with my small group), and had been hoping to experience for years.

9 MY JOB—TO PRAISE GOD

The next year my brother and I began writing songs and lyrics to capture what we felt about our journey of faith—it was a great way to express clearly the depth of our passion:

> Lord, fill me with Your Spirit's might,
> Since I am called by Your great name,
> In You my wandering thoughts unite,
> Of all my works, You are the aim,
> Your love attend me all my days,
> And my sole purpose be Your praise.

× × ×

Longing for you I cry out loud,
Within me a God shaped hole,
I sift my way through the world's crowd,
Till Yours is all my sacred soul,
I dive into Your ocean free
Lost in the open Spirit's sea.

× × ×

Lord Jesus open heaven's doors,
Change my nature into Yours,
Move and spread throughout my soul,
Restart my life and fill me whole.

There were many passages like this that we wrote. I only offer these to show the intensity of our passion for God.

10 THE LIFE OF DISCIPLINE

Later that year, I wrote a letter on the topic: the character of those who want to follow God so much that they make sure they put it into daily practice. I didn't want anyone to reject the ideas before they had read it, so I called it, "The Heart of Daily Christian Living: Disciplined Practice." In this I talked about the perfect Christian life, (making sure that I said before I started, "not that I have already obtained this life myself . . . " just like Paul the apostle said). Here is part of that letter:

This is the character of the people who want to follow God so much that they make sure they put it into daily practice:

They are the kind of people who love the Lord their God with all their heart, all their soul, all their mind, and all their strength. God is the joy of their heart and the desire of their soul. Their inner being is continually crying out, "'Who have I in heaven but You? There is no one on earth I desire more than You.' My God, You are everything to me! 'You are the strength of my heart and all that I have forever.'" That joy comes from spending time with God. They are always content, for they have in them a fountain of water that springs up into everlasting life, and their soul floods over with peace and joy. God's perfect love has swept away all fear from their lives, and they are full of grateful joy all the time. Their joy is so contagious and unstoppable that their whole body seems to say like Peter said, "Praise be to the God and Father of our Lord Jesus Christ! In his great mercy he has given us new birth into a living hope through the resurrection of Jesus Christ from the dead, and into an inheritance that can never perish, spoil or fade— kept in heaven for you" (1 Peter 1:3-4).

Thus, the people who have this living hope are full of eternal life from God. Because of this, they are forever giving thanks. They know that whatever comes their way is not outside of God's will for them in Christ. They believe God is powerful enough to get them through anything. So their motto is: "It's all good! Good is the will of the Lord!" They trust that whether God gives or takes, they can honor His name just the same. Whether they face ease or pain, sickness or health, life or death, they give thanks to God from the bottom of their heart because they trust that God puts everything in order for their good. They put their whole body and soul into God's hands, believing that if He created them and gave them life in the first place, He can certainly take care of them along the way. The people who follow God in daily practice are stressed and full of care about, well, nothing! As they have journeyed, they have lifted the burden of every concern off their backs and handed their cares over to God, knowing that God cares for them. They lean on God for everything, pray to Him regularly, and thank Him endlessly.

Those who follow God in this way live in a constant state of prayer—they don't let their conversation with God come to an end. All the time their heart's voice is saying, "God, my mouth is yours, even when I'm speechless, and even then may my silence speak to you." They are always lifting up prayers to God, at all times and in all places. They don't let anything distract them or prevent them from this inward prayer life—no person or thing can stop them. When they are alone or when they are with friends, at work or play, even in the midst of a conversation with someone—their heart is still with the Lord in prayer. Sleeping or awake, it doesn't matter, God is on their mind. The point is they walk with God every moment of the day! They always keep God in their soul's sight and have trained their eye to see the activity of the invisible God.

Because they spend time in God's presence all day long, the sense that they are deeply loved by God never leaves them. It is easy for them to love God in return. Their hearts overflow, and they are able to love their neighbor as they love themselves. And not just their neighbor—they love every person the same way. They have so embraced God's love for them, that they are able to love even their enemies, and—get this—even the enemies of God himself! And if they find that they are not able to return good to those who do them wrong, they still never fail to pray for them—even when they have been used, rejected, and targeted for harm.

These followers are pure in heart. God's love has washed away all the stains from envy, jealousy, cruelty, anger, rage, and every other bad attitude. Love has scoured away all pride—for pride only brings about disagreement and fights. They have traded these stains for mercy, kindness, gentleness, meekness, humbleness, patience and forgiveness. No one can take from them what they desire—because they don't love the world or anything in it. Instead, all their desires are directed toward God, and their aim is to never forget God—not for one moment.

There is one design and path for their life—to do God's will instead of their own will. Their one intention at all times and in all places is not to please themselves but to please God whom they love. They have a singular focus, and because they do, their whole body is full of light. Their whole life is light—just like when a lamp brightens a whole house. God alone reigns in their hearts; "holiness to the Lord" is the motto of their soul. If they were able to do so, they would not even let their heart beat except that it beat in time to God's will. Every thought that comes to their mind is directed to God, and every thought is made captive to Christ.

Just as the Bible says, "a tree is recognized by its . . . fruit" (Luke 6:44) and those who love God will "keep [his] commandments" (Deuteronomy 5:10), you can tell the character of these people by their lifestyle. They live to follow God's commandments, not just some or most of them, but all of them—from the least to the greatest. Whatever God has put off-limits, they stay away from; whatever God has asked of them, they do. They walk in the path of whatever God says and their steps are not heavy—they have a bounce in their step because their heart is free. They know the honor and joy of obedience, and every day their head is covered with rejoicing. For there is no greater feeling than doing God's "will on earth as it is [done] in heaven" (Matthew 6:10).

They seek to keep all the commandments of God with all their might. Here is the key—their obedience is in proportion to their love. Love is the source that obedience flows from. Therefore, because they love God with all their heart, they serve Him with all their strength; they continually present their soul and body as a living sacrifice, holy and acceptable to God. They give themselves to Him entirely, without reserve, devoting themselves and all they have and all they are to His glory. Whatever abilities they have, they constantly use them to assist their Master in doing His will; they use every power and talent and every part of their body for Him.

So the consequence of putting their faith into daily practice is that everything they do they end up doing for God's glory. In every job and task they have, they not only aim to give God glory (with a single-minded purpose) but they are actually able to do it. At work, at play, or at prayer—everything they are about serves God. Whether they are inside or outside, awake or at rest, they're furthering the one true business of their life. Whether they are getting dressed, are busy at work, are sitting down to eat and drink, or are taking in some form of entertainment, they are advancing the glory of God. This is because wherever they go, their life brings peace and goodwill. The one unchanging rule of their life is this: "Whatever you do, whether in word or deed, do it all in the name of the Lord Jesus, giving thanks to God the Father through him" (Colossians 3:17).

Not even the customs of this world keep them from running the race that is set before them. They have chosen not to follow the world's lifestyle and lay up treasures on earth; they can't do the things that the world does anymore, just as no one can eat fire without getting burned. They can't speak evil of their friends nor can they lie for anyone—including God (or try to justify a lie in the name of God). They can't utter any unkind word about anyone because they use love as the gate that guards their words, stopping the bad ones from leaving their mouths. They don't bother with gossip, or chitchat, and they don't say anything that isn't good or helpful. You have heard the phrase "if you can't say anything good, don't say anything at all," right? Well they don't say anything unless it offers grace to those who hear it. Instead of wasting their words, they take "whatever is true, whatever is noble, whatever is right, whatever is pure, whatever is lovely, whatever is admirable" (Philippians 4:8)—and they think, speak, and do it. In this way, they are able to keep God in all things, every moment of every day.

This was the first time I was able to put into words all that I had been thinking about the perfect Christian life. After thinking through all of this for a few years, it was at this point I decided to become "a man of one book," seeing that nothing could compare to the Bible for my life.

11 FACING OPPOSITION

I don't know that anyone has objected to what I have written to this point, and no serious Christian has objected to the main thrust of it so far. But when I first let this out and it had a chance to circulate, an outcry rose up among some church people—fellow believers, and it shocked me a little. They objected to my use of the word "perfection." They didn't say that what I stated about this perfect life was wrong—they objected to the possibility of perfection at all. They told me, "There is no perfection on earth." They argued strongly against my brother and I for saying otherwise. We never expected such a rough attack from church people, especially since we shared the same views on the vital beliefs of the faith—we agreed that we are made right before God through faith alone, and we clearly stated that all of salvation comes by the grace of God. But what surprised us most was when they said that we had "slammed and put down Christ," by saying that He "saved us the whole way, to the point of making us holy, not leaving anything undone." They had a problem with the fact that we said Christ alone reigns in our hearts, and that He brings everything in our lives under submission to Him.

12 "A Perfect Christian Life"

About a year later, I spoke with Dr. Gibson, who was a key church leader in London. He asked me very directly what I meant when I spoke about "a perfect life." Without trying to hide anything or hold anything back, I explained it to him. When I was finished, he said, "If this is everything you mean when you talk about 'a perfect life,' then tell it to the whole world. If anyone is able to argue against it, let them try." So, I said, "Fine, I will," and I wrote the following, an account of the perfect life in plain language. In it I attempted to explain what the phrase, "a perfect Christian life" means.

First, in what ways are Christians NOT perfect?

Christians are not perfect in knowledge—what we know and understand about the world and about life. We don't know everything, and we are certainly capable of making mistakes. When we talk about a perfect life, we are not expecting every-

23

one to go around without making any mistakes. That's silly. We are human beings, not God. We don't know everything that God knows. Since we don't know every possible outcome of our actions, we can certainly make a mistake when choosing what to do. In addition, Christians are not immune to weaknesses or normal human imperfections. We can be slow to understand; we can be ready with a word at one moment and speechless at another; we can let our imaginations get bogged down in depressing thoughts or let it run away from us. One person may struggle with these things, another may struggle with inappropriate language, have slurred speech, or some other problem. We could think of a thousand defects that each of us carry with us every day, whether in speech, action, or something else. We will not be rid of these human weaknesses until we reach heaven. In the same way, we can't expect to be free from temptation in this life. The Bible says, "A servant [is not] above his master" (Matthew 10:24) and just as Jesus was tempted, we can expect to be tempted as well. Some have been confused, thinking that by perfection I mean "without flaw." Just by being human we can rule that out of our life here on earth! There is no "absolute perfection" here. Neither is there any kind of perfection of degrees, where someone could say, "I'm perfect, to a point." We can't talk about being perfect on some sort of scale, because no matter how far we go up the scale, there are always more steps to climb, always one more way to make ourselves perfect, trying to get closer to "absolute perfection." No, that is not what we are talking about. God doesn't expect that kind of perfection from us. He made us and understands what it means to be a human being.

Second, in what ways ARE Christians perfect?

Now to begin with, when we talk about this idea of living a perfect Christian life, we are not talking about baby Christians, we are talking about mature Christians. Even so, God has given brand-new Christians power not to sin. In this way, they too can live a perfect life in Christ. It's true. We don't *have* to sin. In the Bible, the book of 1 John says this exact point (see 1 John 3:6-9), and there is nothing in the rest of

Scripture that goes against it. Some may argue that even the holiest of God's people in the Old Testament committed sin, to which I say, so what? You can't expect me to believe that just because some saint in the Old Testament sinned, that, therefore, every Christian will and must commit sin as long as they live. It's just not so.

Some people have also tried to use the Bible to say that we can't live a life without sin. They say, "Doesn't the Bible say 'A righteous person sins seven times a day'?" Well, they had better take another look. It says in Proverbs 24:16, "For though a righteous man falls seven times, he rises again." First of all, it doesn't say that this happens seven times *a day*. Second, it doesn't talk about *falling into sin*; it talks about falling. "Falling" is very different from "sinning." In this passage, "fall" could easily mean falling into harm or suffering. The point of the verse is that they don't give up, they get up—not that they must sin.

When that argument doesn't work, they try this one: "But Solomon says in Ecclesiastes, 'There is not a righteous man on earth who does what is right and never sins'" (7:20). We could certainly say that from Solomon's time until Christ there probably wasn't any person who lived and did not sin. But whatever you say about that time when people lived under the Old Testament law, today we have revealed to us Jesus who lived a perfect life without sin. He calls us to be like Him. Since the life and message of Jesus has been given, we can safely affirm what 1 John says, "No one who is born of God will continue to sin" (3:9).

You can't measure the life we enjoy against the experiences of those in the Old Testament. The fullness of God's timing and revelation is here—the Holy Spirit has been given, the wonderful salvation that God offers us has been brought to us by the revelation of Jesus Christ. The kingdom of heaven is now on earth!

"And what about the New Testament? There were saints in the New Testament who sinned (even Peter denied Jesus, and Paul called himself the chief of sinners.)" Are you saying that if two apostles at one time in history committed sin, then all other Christians in all other times are doomed to commit sin as long as they live? No way. We can't say that. The truth is there is no necessity to sin placed upon us. The grace that God gives was enough for Peter and Paul, and it is enough to give us the power to live free from sin today.

What about the passages in 1 John that say, "If we claim to be without sin, we deceive ourselves and the truth is not in us" (1:8), and "If we claim we have not sinned, we make him out to be a liar and his word has no place in our lives" (1:10).

Here is my understanding of these verses: First of all, these verses are not saying that we must sin. Verse 9 helps us understand the other two, "If we confess our sins, he is faithful and just and will forgive us our sins and purify us from all unrighteousness." These verses are saying that the blood of Christ cleanses us from all sin. So the meaning of these verses is this—no person can say, "I don't need the sacrifice of Jesus, I have no sin to be cleansed from." If we say we *have not sinned*, we are trying to fool ourselves, and we make God out to be a liar. If we had no sin to be cleansed from, then why did Christ have to go to the Cross? The final word on the matter is this: Christians are perfect in the sense that God gives them the power to keep from sin.

This is the great opportunity of every Christian, even if they are just beginning in their faith. It is not only possible to say "no" to sin, it is God's goal for the mature believer. As we grow in Christ, God makes us perfect by freeing us from evil thoughts. Where do evil thoughts come from? They come from a person's heart. So, if the heart is no longer evil, then evil thoughts can no longer flow out of it, for "a good tree cannot bear bad fruit" (Matthew 7:18).

And just as people are set free from evil thoughts, they are also freed from evil feelings and emotions. The Christian who is grown up in their faith is able to say like Paul, "I have been crucified with Christ and I no longer live, but Christ lives in me" (Galatians 2:20). These words describe a deliverance from both inward and outward sin. First, when Paul says, "I no longer live" he means the sin-life in him (and us) has received a death sentence and has been executed. Second, he says, "Christ now lives in me," which means that Christ has taken sin's place and now lives in us. Because He lives in us, so does everything holy, right, and good. You can't keep the body of evil in you and try to make room for Christ too. As the Bible says, "What fellowship can light have with darkness?" (2 Corinthians 6:14). They can't coexist. One has got to go.

Those who have allowed Jesus to remove evil from them have "purified their hearts by faith" (Acts 15:9) and have let Christ make their heart His home. You see, when Christ takes up residence in your life, He cleans house. He turns your heart into a home fit for a king. So those who have Christ in them are made pure "just as he is pure" (1 John 3:3). They have the hope of becoming like Jesus in holiness. Here's how it works. Jesus was lowly in heart, so when He comes into your life, He purifies you from all pride. Jesus desired to only do the will of the Father, so when He alone reigns in your life, He makes you pure from selfish desires and self will. Jesus was meek and gentle, so when He makes your heart His home, He cleans out all anger. (You know the kind we are talking about —the bad kind of anger. Jesus himself got angry at hurtful, sinful things, but in His anger, He never stopped loving.)

Jesus saves us from our sins in two ways: He not only saves us from our outward sinful actions, but He also saves us from the inward sinful attitudes and thoughts of the heart. Now, some people will say that "of course this is true, but this doesn't happen until after we have died, not in this life, not in this world." But on the contrary, the Bible says, "In this way, love is made complete among us so that we will have confidence on the Day of Judgment, because *in this world* we are like him" (1 John 4:17, emphasis added). This passage states beyond all doubt that not only in the afterlife, but also in the here and now, "in this world," we are as He is. We are becoming like Him.

Elsewhere, in the same letter, it says, "God is light; in him there is no darkness at all. . . . If we walk in the light, as he is in the light, we have fellowship with one another, and the blood of Jesus, his Son, purifies us from all sin" (1 John 1:5, 7). These verses along with the verse we looked at before, "If we confess our sins, he is faithful and just and will forgive us our sins and purify us from all unrighteousness" (1 John 1:9), are all talking about a deliverance that happens in this world. It doesn't say, the blood of Christ *will* purify you, at the hour of your death, or on the Day of Judgment. Instead it is present tense—His blood *purifies*—now for all Christians who are alive reading those verses. And it doesn't say that we are purified from *some* sin. No, we are purified from *all* sin. So, if there was any speck of sin remaining, the verse could not say that we are purified from *all* sin. If any attitude of unrighteousness stayed with us, we would not be purified from it. Do you see? If we truly believe in this Book, then we are truly made clean! Don't let anyone try to convince you that this passage only relates to being forgiven from sin, and not purified from it. Don't let them tell you that the Bible is only talking about having just your guilt taken away and doesn't apply to removing the *cause* of sin from within you. First John 1:9 has two parts, and it covers both—He is faithful "to forgive us our sin" *and* He "purifies us from all unrighteousness."

Here's the point: Christians are made pure, saved from all sin, and cleansed from all unrighteousness, *in this life*—and that is what we are talking about when we say we are able to live a perfect life. God enables us to stay away from sin, and frees our minds from evil thoughts and our hearts from evil attitudes and desires.

13 Two Works of Grace

About a year later, as my brother and I continued writing songs to God, it became clear that people were still misunderstanding what it meant to live a perfect life. So we decided that it needed further explanation . . .

This great gift of God, the rescuing and saving of our souls, is none other than the image of God freshly stamped on believers' hearts. Salvation is an awakening of believers in spirit and mind. We are awakened to the fact that we are renewed in our likeness to our Creator. He restores us to our original created image. God has put "the axe . . . at the root of the trees" (Matthew 3:10), cutting off any growth of sin in us; He has purified our hearts by faith. His Holy Spirit has made the thoughts of our hearts clean. Because we are pure in heart, we carry with us the hope that we will see God as He really is (Matthew 5:8). With this hope, we keep ourselves pure even as He is pure, and we have become holy "just as he who called [us] is holy" (1 Peter 1:15), keeping every conversation we have pure as well. Not that we have already become all that God is turning us into—we haven't "arrived," and so I wouldn't say we are perfect the way we will be eternally perfect in heaven. But daily we "go from strength to strength" (Psalm 84:7), becoming more and more like Him. Sure we see ourselves through a dingy mirror—the image of what we will become is unclear and cloudy. Nevertheless, we are changing into the original image of Christ that God stamped on us. We are being rebuilt using Christ's blueprint. God's Holy Spirit makes this change in us, shaping us like clay to look perfectly like His Son—and when He does, we look more and more like what God intended us to look like in the first place.

So where the Spirit of the Lord is, there is great freedom—fantastic freedom from the law of sin and death. Unfortunately, the children of this world don't believe it or receive it, even when it is told to them plainly. The Son of God himself has made every one who has been born of God like an escaped prisoner, set free from the chains of sin, bitterness, and pride. Those who daringly live under this freedom understand that they are dependent upon God for everything, and He is their source. Those who trust God in this way put God in the forefront of their thoughts, understanding that He is the One at work in them helping them to will and to act according to His good pleasure. They have a sense that when they talk, it is not them speaking, but God who speaks through them, and that whatever work they do with their hands, it is really the Father in them who is doing the work. In other words, for believers who have placed themselves in total dependence upon

God, He is all in all, He is the central focus of life, and they see themselves as nothing next to Him.

This freedom they enjoy doesn't stop there—they are also set free from self-will, and so they desire nothing but the perfect will of God. They don't long after tons of possessions, seek a pain-free life, or look for fulfillment in life, death, or any created thing on earth. Instead, their heart's cry is always, "not my will, but yours be done" (Luke 22:42). They are set free from evil thoughts, and are so unbelievably free from them that they can't entertain them for even a moment. Before God had done this work in them, an evil thought would pop up in their mind, and they would look up and focus on it for a moment, but now evil thoughts like that don't even pop up. They don't have room for them because their soul is so full of God.

They have spent enough time in prayer that their mind is disciplined—it no longer wanders while they are praying. Whenever they stop for prayer, their mind is not cluttered with anything from their past, their present, or worries of the future; they are able to focus on God alone. In the past, they had wandering thoughts dart in and out of their heads, which came and went like a puff of smoke, but now that smoke no longer rises up to distract them. They are not troubled by overwhelming fear or doubt; they are not concerned about life in general. They don't worry over which course of action to take. They let the Holy Spirit flow over them like holy ointment; He guides the direction of their life, so they don't have to worry about it. In one sense, this perfect life in God has freed them from temptation—although there may be a thousand temptations buzzing around them, they aren't troubled or moved by them. The presence of God in their life allows them to keep an even keel—they stand straight and are unmoved by the pressures of life. They have a supernatural peace and a joyful inner life. They know that God has put His seal on them and a crown awaits them on the day of redemption.

Now don't get me wrong. I'm not saying that those who haven't had this kind of experience are children of the devil and are not Christian. Far from it. Whoever trusts in God and believes that Christ's death has brought the forgiveness of their sins is a child of God. They live in God and will inherit all the promises of God. They should not lose heart because they struggle with temptations. They should take heart, because God is still at work and won't abandon them.

Now we have to understand (lest we give up before we have started) that everything intended for us in this salvation does not happen all at once. There is both an immediate and a gradual component to the work of God. There are plenty of people who have received from God in one instance either a clear sense that their sins were forgiven or the sense of the presence and fullness of the Holy Spirit at rest upon them. But we can't think of anyone who has said that *both* of these things happened to them at the same moment in time. I haven't heard anyone tell me that they received salvation from their sins *and at the same instance* they also received the fullness of the presence of the Holy Spirit and a new, clean heart. So don't give up! It is not as if God has given up on you after He saved you. He is still at work.

Of course we don't know every single way in which God can work in our lives. But in general, we have seen the work of God in the lives of believers follow this path that leads them to a perfect life:

First, those who are trusting in themselves, believing they are righteous and in need of nothing are confronted by the Holy Spirit and the Word of God, which totally lay open their lives—all the things they have done are laid out before them. As a result, they feel lost, distant from God, and in danger of going to hell. In this troubled state, they cry out to God and He tells them that their sins have been taken away and the doors to the kingdom of heaven have been opened to them. They begin to experience righteousness, peace, and joy in the Holy Spirit. Sorrow and pain begin to leave and sin has no more dominion over them. They know that it is through faith in the blood of Christ that they are made right before God and they experience peace. They rejoice in the hope of being changed and in the love God has placed in their hearts.

They stay in this state of peace for several days, or weeks, or months and they figure the war is over. However, eventually some of their old enemies—their old habitual sins and weaknesses—come crawling back. It is in this battle that they may fall. When they are attacked, they are gripped with fear that they're not going to make it. They may even believe that God has forgotten them. Sometimes they are convinced that they deceived themselves into thinking that their sins were forgiven in the first place. They become clouded with a covering of sadness and despair. However, is not long before their Lord comes to their rescue. God sends them the Holy Spirit to comfort them and to affirm that they are children of God. At this point they become like little children—meek, gentle, and teachable.

At that teachable moment, they see for the first time the bottom of their hearts—the true underground world inside them. Up to this point, God has not shown them the depths of their hearts, lest they just give up because of what they see— the true horror chambers of the heart. At this time, they see just how deep their pride is, how hurtfully selfish they can be, and how they harbor within themselves hellish embers of wrong. Yet even in the midst of this difficult exposure of self-knowledge and stumbling, the Spirit of God confirms that they are still a part of God's family, a co-heir with Christ in the inheritance that belongs to the children of God. The whole experience shows them that they are completely unable to help themselves and that they can't fulfill their hunger to be fully renewed in the image of God, in true righteousness and holiness.

God knows the heart and sees their humble desire to be changed. He gives them a single-minded vision and a pure heart; He stamps on them His image and affirms their new identity; He makes them a new creation in Christ Jesus; He moves in and makes His home in their heart; and He brings them into His place of rest.

I have to say that this is the best description I can give of the perfect life I am trying to describe. We made it clear that (1) we have experienced and are teaching about a new life, a life changed by the salvation that God gives; (2) you can only receive this salvation by faith, and the only thing that can keep you from it is unbelief; (3) this faith-life and the salvation which it brings are given by God in an instant; and (4) the moment for this to occur is now—we don't need to wait another moment. For the most part, all Christians are in agreement with this understanding of God's salvation.

14 A Quick Review

Most people seem to reject the idea of a perfect life because they are confused by the definition of "perfection." We have been and are still saying: When we talk about perfection in this life, we are not talking about a state where we are exempt from doing good. (It would be like saying, "I have arrived at perfection and can stop doing anything worthwhile for those around me; I no longer have to obey God's Word.") Also, we are not talking about a kind of "super human perfection" where suddenly we know everything, we no longer make honest mistakes, we no longer face temptation, and we suddenly become immune to any weaknesses or illnesses that are a part of being human.

So, what do we mean when we talk about this perfect life? When we say that a person is "perfect" and living this kind of life, we mean that God has given them the mind that Christ had and has enabled them to walk as Christ walked. We are talking about a person who has been "given clean hands and a pure heart" (Psalm 24:4) or to put it another way, they have been made clean from any filth of flesh and spirit. This person is one who has no reason to stumble, and who, "does not continue to sin" (1 John 5:18). In a spiritual sense a "perfect" person is one in whom God has fulfilled His faithful word, "I will cleanse you from all your filthiness and from all your idols . . . I will deliver you from all your uncleanness" (Ezekiel 36:25, 29, NKJV). We know this person to be sanctified through and through—their whole being has been cleansed and set apart for God's use. They walk in the light as He is in the light, and there is no darkness in them, and the blood of Jesus Christ the Son of God has cleansed them from all sin.

A couple of years later, we had several conferences of preachers and teachers where we talked seriously about what the Bible meant by sanctification, which we had termed "perfection." There were many questions tossed around; the answers we gave are as follows:

Q: What does it mean to be sanctified?

A: It means to be renewed in the image of God, "in true righteousness and holiness" (Ephesians 4:24). When we are renewed in the image of God, we become what we were created to be. God cleanses and purifies us from all sin and rebellion in our hearts, and gives us the power to live for Him. We become more like His Son, Jesus, and no longer desire to sin; instead we want to do God's will. The word sanctification simply means "to make holy, to set apart for a holy purpose."

Q: What is implied in being a perfect Christian?

A: To love God with all your heart, mind, and soul (Deuteronomy 6:5). When we love God with everything, we love the things He loves, and we want to do the things He is doing. That's what the Bible means by "be holy because I . . . am holy" (Leviticus 19:2). It is an expression of our love. To live the perfect life means that we love God to the extent that we want to live for Him and be like Him—so the desire to sin has been washed away and replaced by pure love for God.

Q: Does this mean that all inner-life sins are taken away?

A: With all certainty, yes. Otherwise, how can we say that we have been "saved from all our uncleanness"? (Ezekiel 36:29).

Q: When does the inner work of sanctification (being cleansed and set apart for God's use) begin?

A: It starts when a person receives the salvation from sin that God offers. (But sin remains in them; the seed of all sin is still there until they are sanctified, or washed, through and through.) From that beginning point, a believer gradually dies to sin and grows in God's grace.

Q: Isn't this sanctification thing something that happens to believers just a short while before they die?

A: If you don't expect to be cleansed until death, then you probably won't be cleansed until then. The Bible says, "You have not because you ask not" (see James 4:2). God has set things up for us to be in constant communication and dependence upon Him. He says, "Ask and you will receive" (John 16:24). Those who don't ask until later in life, won't receive it until later.

Q: Should we expect to be sanctified sooner?

A: Why not? There may be examples of people who were not sanctified until late in life, and the people who received Paul's letters may not have yet been, and even Paul himself may not claim to be—but none of these things show that we can't be sanctified today. God's power is available now, all we have to do is seek and ask.

Q: How should we talk about sanctification?

A: We should always speak of sanctification in terms of God's promise. We should talk about sanctification by invitation, never through pressure. And we should never make someone feel "imperfect" if they have not yet received all that God has for them.

Q: What about those who disagree with us on this idea of "sanctification"? Are there key areas where we might be able to agree?

A: We all should at least affirm these basic ideas: (1) that every person is sanctified entirely, through and through, before they go to be with God—so everyone who believes will be completely sanctified, if not in this life, then at least in death; (2) that up until the point of death, a believer grows in grace daily and comes nearer and nearer to perfection every day; and (3) that everyone should be continually seeking after this perfect life of being totally cleansed from sin, and they should also encourage others to pursue it as well.

Because of the different ways the word "sanctification" is used in the Bible, to avoid confusion, we will use the term "entire sanctification" or "wholly cleansed" or some other term like that when we are talking about the process of the perfect life, being cleansed from all sin. So when we say "entire sanctification" we mean being completely and wholly cleansed from sin, within and without, made holy and enabled to follow God in a "perfect life" where we are not overpowered by sin, but enabled to walk with God as Jesus walked. We also agree that when we talk with someone, we should only talk about the idea of being "entirely sanctified" after we have first discussed what it means to be saved, or "justified." Just like with children, being born anew into a life with God comes first— growing up and being able to walk straight comes later.

It is also important to affirm that we can expect to live in holiness in this life. Although some may disagree, we believe that God certainly has the power and the desire to enable us to be clean and live a "perfect life," made holy and free from sin, while here on earth.

Q: Is there any promise in Scripture that God will save us from all sin?

A: Of course there is. To start, consider this example: Psalm 130:8 says, "[God] himself will redeem Israel from all their sins." This idea is expressed again in Ezekiel, "I will sprinkle clean water on you, and you will be clean; I will cleanse you from all your impurities and from all your idols. . . . I will save you from all your uncleanness" (36:25, 29). It doesn't get any clearer than that. What a promise! And in reference to this, Paul the apostle encourages us, "Since we have these promises, dear friends, let us purify ourselves from everything that contaminates body and spirit, perfecting holiness out of reverence for God" (2 Corinthians 7:1). Here is another clear and simple ancient promise, "The LORD your God will circumcise your hearts and the hearts of your descendants, so that you may love him with all your heart and with all your soul, and live" (Deuteronomy 30:6). (Circumcision was a physical, irreversible ritual that symbolized commitment and dedication to God. For God to "circumcise our hearts" meant He was spiritually making us able to live out our commitment to Him.)

Q: Are there more New Testament passages that say similar things about this perfect life or about being made holy in this way?

A: Of course there are, and they express it in simple, easy-to-understand terms. Take 1 John 3:8, "He who does what is sinful is of the devil, because the devil has been sinning from the beginning. The reason the Son of God appeared was to destroy the devil's work." Christ came to completely knock down everything the devil tried to set up, without exception, and certainly all sin is from the work of the devil. Paul also talks about this when he writes, "Christ loved the church and gave himself up for her to make her holy . . . to present her to himself as a radiant church, without stain or wrinkle or any other blemish, but holy and blameless" (Ephesians 5:25-27). And he makes a similar statement in Romans 8:3-4, "And so he condemned sin in sinful man, in order that the righteous requirements of the law might be fully met in us, who do not live according to the sinful nature but according to the Spirit."

Consider this verse in Ephesians, "that you may be filled to the measure of all the fullness of God" (3:19). Here the writer prays that we would be so filled with the love of Christ, in mind and heart, that it would give us inner strength, and that we could be filled with all the fullness of God. Think about it—how would our lives be different if we had "the measure of all the fullness of God" in us? I think that if I had God's Spirit working in me that way, then I would have the power to live a perfect life of holiness before the Lord. (Can we have all God's fullness and still harbor sin in our hearts? I believe He gives us the power to kick sin out.) The last example is found in 1 Thessalonians,

"Now may the God of peace himself sanctify you completely; and may your whole spirit, soul, and body be preserved blameless at the coming of our Lord Jesus Christ" (5:23, NKJV). Here the prayer is very direct and easy to understand. He even uses the term, "sanctify . . . completely!" Another way to say it is, "sanctify . . . through and through" (NIV). This is what we have been talking about! It is through this process that we are made blameless for the coming of the Lord Jesus.

One of the New Testament *commands* concerning the perfect life is "Be perfect, therefore, as your heavenly Father is perfect" (Matthew 5:48). It doesn't get any more direct than that. God calls us to live a perfect life. But it is not about human effort—it says our reason, motivation, and power to be perfect are all from God.

Q: Can you explain why you think this process happens before a person dies?

A: There are two main reasons. First, the very nature of the command to live this kind of life is given to the living, not the dead! When God says, "Love [Me] with all your heart" (Matthew 22:37), I don't think He is saying, "Thou shalt do this when you are dead." No, He is calling us to love Him wholly and completely while we are alive; nothing else, including sin, should get in the way. Second, the Scriptures explain this idea very plainly. For example, Titus 2:11-14 says, "For the grace of God that brings salvation has appeared to all men. It teaches us to say 'No' to ungodliness and worldly passions, and to live self-controlled, upright and godly lives in this present age, while we wait for the blessed hope—the glorious appearing of our great God and Savior, Jesus Christ, who gave himself for us to redeem us from all wickedness and to purify for himself a people that are his very own, eager to do what is good." Another example is found in Luke 1:69, 72-75, "He has raised up a horn of salvation for us . . . to show mercy to our fathers and to remember his holy covenant, the oath he swore to our father Abraham: to rescue us from the hand of our enemies, and to enable us to serve him without fear in holiness and righteousness before him all our days."

Q: Are there any examples in Scripture of people who attained this perfect life you describe?

A: The apostle John would be one, and all others he described when he wrote, "Love has been perfected among us in this: that we may have boldness in the day of judgment; because as He is, *so are we* in this world" (1 John 4:17, NKJV, emphasis added).

Q: Can you show us an example of someone today who has been made perfect?

A: To those who ask a question like this, someone might answer, "If I knew of one here, I would not tell you because you are not asking in love. You are like King Herod at the time of Jesus; you only ask to see the young child so you may slay Him—you only ask to see perfection so that you can tear it down."

But, I will answer the question directly—there aren't many, if any, to whom we could point and say, "There is one who lives this perfect life." There are many reasons for this. How could we point to any person and say, "Here is an example of perfection!"? Putting them on that kind of pedestal would be like painting a target on their back and letting people shoot at them. It would be horrible to be in that position and would certainly bring confusion or something worse. People might misunderstand, and seeing some normal human imperfection or flaw in them, throw out the whole idea that God can make us holy. That would be a tragedy. (It would be very easy, but very pointless to just become the critics, who do nothing but rip others apart. As the Bible says, "If they do not listen to Moses and the Prophets"—or Jesus and His apostles, I might add— "they will not be convinced even if someone rises from the dead" [Luke 16:31].) Christian perfection is not about setting up a museum where we can point to statues of those who are perfect. It is about being pure in the inner thoughts, attitudes, and motivations of the heart—having a holy love. A dynamic life like that is hard to point at—it is more like a motion picture than a snapshot.

Q: Isn't it natural to react negatively toward anyone who says they are "saved from all sin?"

A: Yes, this is sad, but true. It happens for many reasons. Sometimes, we are concerned about the people who might get hurt if they find out that a person who says they are saved from all sin is not what they claim to be. Sometimes we don't like hearing that phrase because of a built in envy we have toward people who speak of some "higher achievement" than what we have reached. Sometimes we don't like to hear about things like this because our hearts are slow and not ready to believe the works of God.

Q: Why can't we continue in the joy of our faith until we are perfected in love?

A: There is no reason not to continue in the joy of faith as we go along. "Holy grief" and longing for holiness do not diminish the joy we have in Christ—even while we are under the cross and partake in the sufferings of Christ, we are still filled with joy unspeakable. Let our joy carry us to a deeper love, until we become like Jesus himself, perfect in joy and holiness.

16 Thoughts on Perfection

In all our writings, we never changed what we thought and taught or how we felt about this experience of Christian perfection. And without exception, to this day we have maintained that:

1. Christian perfection is fully loving God and loving your neighbor and being completely delivered by God from all sin;
2. This is received by mere faith—believing that God has the power and desire to make you holy;
3. We believe that this can be given to a believer instantaneously, in a single moment; and

4. We are to expect this perfect way of living, living in this perfect obedience and perfect holiness—not at death, but every moment. Now is as good a time as any, for today is the day of salvation, and God has complete power to bring perfect holiness, this "entire sanctification," to our lives right now.

As we talked with others, we began to notice that there were quite a few different opinions and beliefs about the idea of Christian perfection, so we thought it would be wise to once again collect our thoughts and write them down so that there would be no confusion. A short while later I published an article titled, "Thoughts on Christian Perfection." What follows are some of those ideas, such as this preface to the article:

All I intend to do here is to declare my thoughts and feelings straight up and to the point. I want to explain what the perfect life is, and what it is not, and explain this idea of Christian perfection. Since these thoughts were first a collection of frequently asked questions, I have left them in that format.

Q: What is the perfect life, which is sometimes referred to as Christian perfection?

A: The perfect life is loving God with all your heart, mind, soul, and strength. This implies that no wrong attitude or motive, nothing counter to love remains in the soul. All thoughts, words, and actions come from pure love. Your heart no longer desires to sin but instead desires to live for God in obedience to Him.

(Think of it like this: A dog and its master are playing by the side of a busy road. The dog is running back and forth, through its master's legs, playing and jumping. The dog loves to spend time with its owner, and to play, and while it's running around its master's legs, it is always looking up to him. With every step, the dog turns its head to look at the master. The dog never takes its eyes off its master. Now you can say that the dog would be safer on a leash, but this dog is in no danger of running out into the street—its complete attention and love is for its master, and it has no thought of running away from its master into the street and into danger. That is what we mean when we say that the perfect life is loving God with all your heart, soul, and mind.)

Q: When you say perfection, do you mean that a person is no longer capable of any weaknesses, lack of knowledge, or mistakes?

A: We have never said this, and never will. When we use the term perfection, we don't mean "beyond human." We mean that God removes all sin in you and cleanses you from all unrighteousness, making you perfect in your ability "to will and . . . act according to his good purpose" (Philippians 2:13). You are still a created human being, capable of weakness, sickness, misunderstandings, and honest mistakes.

Q: But how can a person have every thought, word, and action come from pure love, and at the same time make stupid mistakes?

A: I know this is difficult to see, but there is no contradiction here. A person can be filled with pure love and still make mistakes. I don't expect anyone will be free of actual mistakes until we trade these mortal bodies for eternal ones. It is a natural consequence of living as a human being in a limited body. As long as our minds exist in a physical brain, there will be days when our thinking will be off because we are battling a headache. We stub our toe, our emotions change, and we get angry. We can't avoid it while we are in these fallen bodies.

Let's take this a step farther. A mistake in thinking can lead to a mistake in action. There was a man who thought the only way that he could get rid of the desires of the flesh was by causing physical discomfort that would distract him from evil thoughts. His thinking led him to a mistake in practice— wearing an iron girdle! (Talk about discomfort!) This is just one of a thousand examples where our thinking gets twisted and leads to some strange act, even for those who are walking in God's grace. But where every word and action comes from love, a mistake like this is not the same as going out and intentionally committing a sin against someone.

There are many people who agree completely when we talk about this perfect life involving the highest degree of love, but they won't hear of any talk about living without sin. They know very well that all human beings are liable to make mistakes, both in practice and in their thoughts and judgments. But what they do not know, or don't see, is that this is not always a sin. This kind of mistake is not sin if love is the underlying foundation.

Q: If people are without sin, they don't really need Jesus to die for their sins, so doesn't that make Jesus obsolete?

A: Far from it. Those who are walking the path of the perfect life know better than anyone that they need Christ. They know what it's like to be so entirely dependent upon Him that they can't imagine a life without Him. Jesus doesn't give life to our souls apart from himself—He gives life in and with himself. His words are true for all people, no matter what state of grace they are in: "No branch can bear fruit by itself; it must remain in the vine. Neither can you bear fruit unless you remain in me . . . apart from me you can do nothing" (John 15:4-5).

No matter where we are in our journey, no matter what state we are in, we need Christ. All grace is a free gift from Him. His grace is free to us, but it was not cheap; He paid for it with His suffering and with His life. Don't think of this grace as just coming *from* Jesus, we find it *in* Him. For our perfection isn't like a tree, where we get our nourishment from our own roots, rather our perfection is like a branch which is connected to the tree and grows from it. If we are cut off from the tree, we will dry up and die. Anything that strays from God's perfect law needs to be made right and receive the forgiveness of God. But some of these human mistakes and imperfections may not be considered sins. Think about what Paul says in Romans, "Love does no harm to its neighbor. Therefore love is the fulfillment of the law" (13:10). Now mistakes, weaknesses or illnesses that flow out of our broken bodies and

43

do not go against love are not sin according to what we find in this Scripture.

Let me explain a little bit more on this point.

- Let's say there are two kinds of sin—intentional and unintentional. Intentional sin is willfully and voluntarily breaking a known law. For example, Marie takes her car and runs over John on purpose just because she is angry at him. That is murder. Unintentional sin is accidentally or involuntarily breaking one of God's laws, known or unknown to you at the time. For example, Robert hits Julie with his car—he didn't see her because the sun was in his eyes. Robert may kill Julie, but it is not murder. Both kinds of sin need to be made right (in a court of law) and are in need of forgiveness (by both God and the families of the victims).

- Perfection doesn't mean that you will be exempt from unintentional, involuntary wrongs. It doesn't mean you will never make mistakes. I believe that these unintentional actions are a natural consequence of our human mistakes and limitations. They can't be separated from being human. In other words, perfection doesn't mean that you will never get into a car accident. It means that if you live in this pure love for God and others, you won't be overcome by road rage and try to run someone off the road when they cut you off. Instead, you would act out of love, forgive them, let your anger subside, and go on your way.

If you choose to call every mistake a sin, be aware that you run the risk of confusing willful sin with the accidents and flaws of being human. I fear that if we start calling everything a sin, the idea of the perfect life will get watered down and cast aside. If normal human mistakes are sins, and the perfect life by definition is being able to live a holy life and by God's power choose not to sin, then no human could ever live that life, for we can't choose not to make mistakes as human beings!

Q: How can we keep from thinking that this perfect life is more or less than it really is?

A: We can avoid this by keeping the Bible in front of us at all times; we need to set this idea of the perfect life in God as high as the Scriptures put it. It is no higher or lower than fully and completely loving God and people—loving God with our whole heart and people at least as much as we love ourselves. The perfect life is a life that has love flowing through all our thoughts, words, and deeds.

Q: What if someone is able to live the perfect life, should they tell others about it?

A: At first it may seem like they can't hold it in—there is a fire within them and they burn to tell others of God's great mercy. But it would be best not to go up to people who don't know God and say, "Hey, I'm perfect." They would just argue or try to contradict them, or worse, say bad things about them and the work that God is doing in them. There is no reason to say anything about it to anyone unless something good will come of it. And then, we should be very careful not to brag about it, as if it was something we had done for ourselves. Instead whenever we talk about it, we should do so with humility, giving God the respect and honor due Him.

When believers get a chance to talk to others about a deeper walk, it helps the listeners grow; it gives them focus for their own journey and increases their hunger and thirst to go deeper themselves. If we stayed quiet, other believers would not have that benefit.

Q: What reasonable proof can we see that shows God is at work in a person? How can we know with certainty that someone is saved from all sin?

A: We cannot know with all certainty that someone has been saved from all sin, nor can we know that someone is saved period. Unless God gives us miraculous insight, we can't know for sure. However, there are several things that most people would agree are suitable proof and would leave little room for doubt:

- If we can see clear evidence of the change in a person's

life and actions long before he or she begins to tell others of the change, then we have reason to believe that God is at work and they are not trying to "lie for God." They are not trying to appear spiritual by claiming that they have experienced something that they have not actually experienced.

- If this person can give a clear account of the time and the way in which the change took place, then we who hear it can verify what he or she has to say, and see if it is consistent with the ways we know God works.
- If all of this person's actions following the time when he or she claims to have been cleansed are holy and blameless, then it is likely that the claim is true.

Here is another quick way to affirm this work when someone says they have been cleansed from all sin:

- We have confidence in this person's character and believe he or she will not lie.
- The person testifies before God saying, "I feel no sin, but everything in me is love. I pray, rejoice, and give thanks constantly and at all times. I have a clear and real sense in my spirit that I am completely renewed, and I have been made right with God. I stand in a state of being saved and cleansed."
- If we have no reason to oppose what this person says, then we ought to believe that God has done a great work in him or her.

It doesn't do us any good to say, "But I know of mistakes that this person has made, they can't be perfect." We have already said that this idea of perfection is not talking about making mistakes.

Q: But what if a person who claims to have this perfection is surprised by a noise, or falls down, or is scared by some sudden danger? Doesn't that show that they are not perfect?

A: Not at all. On the outside, you can be startled, scared silly, or embarrassed to the point that you turn red, while on the inside your soul is still and calm before God, relaxing in His perfect peace. Your mind can be deeply distressed, sorrowed, stumped, weighed down, or even anguished, but your heart can be wrapped tightly around God in perfect love. You can in the midst of life's uncertainties be submitted to God's will. Didn't Jesus' life portray that? Has anyone faced the kind of anguish, agony, and distress that He faced? And, yet, He was without sin.

Q: Can anyone who has a pure heart enjoy the taste of good food or seek all kinds of pleasure from their senses? If so, how are they any different from everyone else?

A: The difference between them is this: the pure in heart don't need any of these pleasures to make them happy—their happiness comes from within, not through their senses. They see and love God, and their life overflows with gratitude. They may use their senses and enjoy what they see, hear, taste, and smell, but they don't seek after them as if that was their main goal in life. They take in life's enjoyments sparingly, in moderation, and not for the sake of the thing itself. So, in the case of food, of course they will prefer good tasting food to bland food. The difference is that they can eat without the danger of getting caught up in empty pleasure seeking. They understand that God gives us all things to richly enjoy and that is where their focus is—on giving thanks to God. So to them, the smell of a flower, the taste of grapes, and all life's pleasures serve to expand their delight in God who made them. So just because people become perfected in love doesn't mean that they can't get married or get a job that they have skills for—they are actually in a great position to go about living, for they are now able to go about life and work without hurry or worry and without any distraction in their spirit.

Some people might say, "But this person does not live up to my idea of a perfect Christian." It is possible that no one ever will because these people's idea of a perfect Christian may go beyond any scriptural account. Their thoughts on Christian perfection may include more than the Bible includes, or they may include something that the Bible does not. A scriptural idea of perfection is pure love filling the heart and controlling all words and actions. If anyone's idea of perfection includes anything more or anything else, it is not scriptural, and it is no wonder that no one can live up to it.

I fear that many people stumble on this point. They include all kinds of ingredients that are found nowhere in Scripture. They create their own idea of Christian perfection from their own imagination, and then they disregard anyone who does not live up to their imaginary standard.

We should take great care to keep this simple, scriptural account of what the perfect life actually is in front of our eyes. The Bible's whole idea of Christian perfection can be summed up in this way—pure love reigning as the only king on the throne of our heart and life.

Q: What if two perfect Christians have children? Since there is no sin in them, their children would be born without sin, right?

A: This is a tricky question that relates to what we believe about the nature of sin and where it comes from. I don't think we will ever see something like this. Here is why—sin is fixed upon us, not by our mother or father, but by our first parent—Adam. The Bible says that "in Adam all die" (1 Corinthians 15:22), and "through the disobedience of the one man the many were made sinners" (Romans 5:19). All of us, without exception, are the offspring of the one who ate the forbidden fruit. So the seed of sin is passed on to us because we are all fallen human beings—it is not something that can skip a generation—as if we could inherit holiness from our parents the same way we get our eye or hair color. As human beings we are fallen, regardless of the failings of our parents.

Q: When can people say they have attained the perfect life?

A: People can say they have attained the perfect life when they first become convinced that sin is not just something they do, but it is something that comes from a corruption of the heart. When this happens, people experience a deeper and clearer conviction than they had experienced when they were saved. Their heart is pierced and it leads them to become more uncomfortable with the presence of sin, until God brings about a total death to sin. Then they become entirely renewed in love and in the image of God. They are overjoyed all the time; they pray without ceasing; they give thanks in everything. This is not to say that feeling "all love and no sin" is proof of the perfect life. Many people have felt this way before they came to the place where they were fully renewed. So no one should think that this work of God is finished in them until it is confirmed by the Holy Spirit. God's own Spirit will be a witness to the fact that sin has been completely cleaned out of their lives. Then their entire sanctification is as easy to recognize as their salvation.

Q: Does it ever happen that some imagine they are sanctified when in reality they're not?

A: It does happen, but only when they don't look within themselves to see all the marks and qualities that we have just mentioned. Instead they either judge themselves by only some of these qualities or they judge themselves by some other qualities that are vague and made up. I don't know of any instance of when a person had all the marks of these experiences and wasn't sanctified. So if David had this complete experience, he probably wasn't mistaken to think that God was making him pure. I don't know if it's possible to possess all of the things we have been talking about and not be cleansed from all sin. So, (for example) after David is saved, he becomes deeply and fully convinced that his nature is still sinful deep within, and he experiences a gradual denial, rejection, and painful death of sin in him, and he experiences an entire renewal of himself in the image of God, and his life is changed in a great way—and added to this is a clear direct witness of the renewal—then I don't think he would be deceived to think of himself as completely washed and sanctified by God. And if people told me that this was their experience, I would not reject what they told me without a very good reason.

Q: Is this death to sin and renewal in love gradual or instantaneous?

A: People may be dying for some time and yet not "die" until the soul is separated from the body. In that instant, they live the eternal life. In the same way, we may be dying to sin for some time and yet not be dead to sin until it is separated from our soul. In that instant, we live the perfect life—the full life of love, where we will to do God's will and have only love in our hearts for God and others. When we die, our bodies go through a change, becoming a different kind of body, greater than any we have known here on Earth. It is such a new and different body, and a new and different existence, that we can't even fathom what it will be like until we get there. And so it is when the soul dies to sin—we enter into a different kind of life, one greater than we have ever known before. It is such a new and different existence that we cannot imagine what it will be like until we experience it. Having said all that, we will always be growing in grace, in the knowledge of Christ, and in the love and image of God—and will continue to do so all the way up until we die. After that, who knows? Perhaps we will continue to grow all the more.

Q: How do we wait for this change to happen?

A: For the sake of God don't wait in careless indifference as if holiness doesn't matter, and don't wait in dulled inactivity, doing nothing. Instead, keep your energy and drive, walk in total obedience, not neglecting any of God's commandments. Wait in watchfulness, denying yourself, and taking up your cross every day. Keep on in earnest prayer and fasting, with careful attention to the word of God. Don't think you can attain this change by some other means—by doing nothing and having it plop on your lap or by working so hard that you climb your way up the ladder of perfection. (And don't think that you will be able to hold on to it in that way either!) The change that comes happens by simple faith. But it is like a partnership—God asks us to seek Him, and as we seek Him with everything, He does His part and provides for our every need and grants us even the faith that we need to be changed.

Ask yourself, "How many are seeking God in this way and seeking holiness with a determined passion?" So few have received the blessing of this changed, perfect life because so few have decided they wanted it enough to seek God for it. God is waiting, but He asks us to walk in faith and seek Him!

Take prayer for example. There are few who are willing to take the time to pray or wrestle with God, seeking the blessing of perfection. That's the problem, we "do not have, because [we] do not ask" (James 4:2) or worse, because we "ask with wrong motives" (James 4:3). Talk about wrong motives, I know of some who ask that they would be renewed just before they die. *Just before they die!* "Please, God, make me holy someday, sometime, way down the road." Would that make them happy? Why don't they ask for it now, today, while it is still called today? They say they don't want to force God into their timeline. Give me a break! Why wouldn't it be God's will for them to be holy as He is holy *now*? Today and tomorrow are His time. Hurry up! What are you waiting for? Let your soul pursue the perfect life, and let your heart be on fire for the love of God.

Q: Can we continue in peace and joy until we're perfected in love?

A: Of course we can! The kingdom of God is not divided against itself; it is not as if we're fighting against God. We shouldn't let anything discourage us from rejoicing in the Lord always. We may feel great pain in our struggle against the sin nature that remains in us. But this should not bring us sorrow; instead it should spur us on to depend upon God more and more every moment as our strong helper. Every day we more earnestly "press on toward the goal to win the prize for which God has called [us] heavenward in Christ Jesus" (Philippians 3:14). And when the sense of sin is overwhelmingly great, the sense of His love all around us will be even greater.

Q: How should we treat those who think they have attained the perfect life?

A: We should take a close look at their lives and encourage them to pray with intensity that God would show them all that is in their hearts. Throughout the New Testament those who are full of grace and are intently seeking God are given sincere encouragement to allow God's grace to abound in their lives, and at the same time, they are given the strongest caution to avoid every kind of evil. But if we are to offer any kind of challenge or caution, we should do it with gentle tenderness and without any harshness, sternness, or bitterness of tongue. We should be careful not to injure them with even the appearance of anger or unkindness. It is the job of the devil and his demons to tempt, not ours. So when we speak to someone like Lisa about her life, we should relax, and remember that if she is faithful to the grace that God has given her, then she is in no danger of stumbling or perishing.

Q: But what harm can it do if we deal with them harshly?

A: Remember we're talking about those who feel they have attained the perfect life. Either they have attained it or they have not. If they are mistaken, and we deal harshly with them, it may crush them. They may become so discouraged that they sink and are unable to get back up. If they're not mistaken, then we may grieve those whom God has not grieved. If they are actually full of His Spirit, treating them unkindly or with contempt is going against the Spirit of God. We wouldn't be doing them any good, and in fact, we would be hurting ourselves! It would not be good to foster an improper attitude in ourselves by critiquing others. What kind of self-righteous, self-sufficient attitude is behind the desire to set ourselves up as some sort of Spanish Inquisition, the self-assured judges over the deep things of God? Seriously, are we qualified for that work? Can we pronounce, in every case, how deep people's sins are and how much God has washed away, and how much of His love He has put there? Can we precisely determine how God's work in their lives will influence their appearance, movement, or tone of voice? If we can do all that, then we are the wisest who ever lived.

Q: But if those who claim to have the perfect life are displeased that we don't believe them, isn't that proof against them that they really don't have it?

A: It depends. If they are angry, it would tend to be proof that they are not living in perfection, but if they are grieved in their spirit that we don't believe them, then it doesn't prove anything. They have a right to be grieved if we don't believe and don't rejoice in a legitimate work of God. It is also true that we could easily mistake their grief for anger, and then we have judged them in error.

Q: Isn't it a good thing to find out and expose those who think they have attained the perfect life when they actually have not?

A: It is only a good thing to find this out in a mild, gentle way, by asking in love. We are not in a game where we get points for how many "false perfects" we can find and expose. It would be wrong to get excited or joyful if we found someone who was mistaken on this matter. Instead, shouldn't we be overwhelmed with grief, concern, and tears? Here is one who seemed to be living proof of God's power to save us to the ultimate—but it is not as we hoped. They "have been weighed and found wanting" (Daniel 5:27). And you think this is cause for joy? I think we should only rejoice, and rejoice greatly, if we find a person full of pure love, who is exactly as they say they are. That is cause for joy.

"But they shouldn't call themselves perfect when they are not, if they do, they are fooling themselves." So what? What if they have been happily going along, and they have misunderstood, or they really don't have all their sin yet removed. It is a harmless mistake, and they have been going along in life full of love. Even if they got it wrong, they still have been living with much grace, much holiness, and much happiness. We might not rejoice in an honest mistake, but I would get pretty excited to see people living as close as they can to

God's call for their lives. It is a happy occasion when someone is full of Christian joy, prayer and thanksgiving, has no bad attitudes, and loves God all the time. I would continue to rejoice, if sin is minimized until it is completely destroyed.

Q: Isn't it dangerous for people to think that they have attained perfection when they haven't yet?

A: As long as they feel free from sin (whether it has actually been totally erased yet or not), they are in no danger. Remember what we said before. Sometimes people have an experience of renewal and joy and feel free from sin, but they have not yet been fully cleansed (or as we say, entirely sanctified). Sure there was danger before and there will be again when they face new trials and temptations, but while love is filling their thoughts, words, and actions, they are in no danger. They are happy and safe under God's care as He brings them through the process of making them holy. Let them continue in the experience of renewed love as long as they can! Don't put the fire out! If we must do something, then we can remind them of the dangers to come—that their love might grow cold, or sin may come back and rise up again. It would be good to remind them not to throw away hope—they should not assume that because they have not yet attained this life that they never will.

Q: But what if nobody has attained this perfect life yet? What if everyone who thinks so is deceived?

A: If you can convince me of this, then I will stop speaking and writing about it (and you can put this book down!). But understand this—truth is not built on this person or that person. This person or that person may be deceived, but I would not change my way of thinking. However, if there really is no one who has yet been made perfect, and no real evidence of it, then any further talk of it is pointless.

Consider another idea that is similar to it. You have heard there is a "peace of God, which passes all understanding" (Philippians 4:7). If you can convince me that this statement is powerless, and that in all these years there is no one who has ever experienced this peace, and no one alive who is living in it—then I will stop teaching about it. We can, however, be fairly certain that it is true based on the stories of those who have gone before us.

Q: What does it matter whether anyone has attained it or not, seeing that there are many references to this idea in Scripture?

A: If I were convinced that there was no one alive who was living this perfect life, even though it had been taught by many for a long time, I would then assume that we had all been mistaken and had misunderstood the meaning of the Scriptures. If I were convinced of that, then I would change my teaching, and teach instead that "sin stays with us until death."

17 THE DANGER OF FANATICISM

Several years later, the work of the Spirit of God in our midst and in our city greatly increased. Many who formerly didn't care about spiritual things were deeply convinced that they were lost and needed God; many found redemption in the blood of Christ. Many who had been backsliders (those who had fallen away from their faith) were changed and came back to the faith. There were also a large number of people who believed God had saved them from all sin. Knowing how the devil tries to mess up the work of God, I was very careful to make them aware of the dangers, especially pride and allowing their emotions to get carried away in spiritual excitement. While I was there with them, they continued to stay humble and clearheaded. But as soon as I left, there were many that got carried away with emotional enthusiasm. Two or three began to mistake their own imaginations for visions from God. They got the idea that they would never die, and they tried to convince others to join them in their thinking. It caused much confusion among the believers. Then they got some others to believe with them that they could not be tempted and that they would never again feel any pain. They began to think that they could see into the future and that they could tell when someone had a demon. By the time I came back, some of them had calmed down, come to their senses, and checked their ideas against the Bible, but others were beyond help and would not listen to sound teaching. I began to take criticism on every side—from those who said I corrected them too much and from those who said I did not correct them enough. However, God's Spirit continued to work among us, and more and more of those who were far from God came to know Him. Almost daily there were people coming to receive salvation; there were also many who were enabled to love Him with all their hearts.

18 THE CHALLENGE OF OPPOSITION

About this time I received a letter from a friend who helped me think through my circumstances of challenges and opposition. He wrote:

Don't be alarmed that Satan sows "weeds among the wheat" (Matthew 13:25) of Christ. It has always been the way the devil works, and he will always work that way. The devil will always try to counteract the work of the Spirit of Christ. An effect of the devil's work is that he will use people to openly ridicule the work of God to discourage the faithful.

What can real Christians do? They should live worthy of their name and pray that those who have been led from truth into error may be delivered. They should seek to reclaim them with a spirit of gentleness. Most importantly, these true believers should not let the attacks of the enemy or discouragement of others steal their hunger for complete holiness of body, soul, and spirit—for "without holiness no one will see the Lord" (Hebrews 12:14).

This idea of becoming a completely new creature in Christ is just madness to a mad world. But it is the will and wisdom of God—and may we all seek after it!

But there are some who teach the fullness of this perfect life who are often guilty of limiting the Almighty God. He gives out His gifts as He pleases—so we dare not say that you must be a Christian for a certain period of time before you can receive this Spirit of holiness. God's usual methods are one thing—but what He will do in His good pleasure is another. He has wise reasons for speeding up and for slowing down His work. Sometimes He moves suddenly and unexpectedly, and at other times, we don't see Him until we have been looking for Him for a long time.

I have thought for some time that the reason why people don't see more of a movement of God in their own life is because of their own coldness of heart, neglect, and unbelief. It is sad to think that that this is true of believers.

May Christ's Spirit give us good judgment in all things and fill us "with all the fullness of God" (Ephesians 3:19, NKJV) so that we "may be perfect and complete, lacking nothing" (James 1:4, NKJV).

19 For Those Who Say We Can't

Some questions that came out of some of these arguments and criticisms led one simple, regular Christian man to write out some questions of his own . . . (though some of these were really statements of faith, put in the form of a question to challenge the thinking of those who argued against us):

Here are some questions that I humbly proposed to those who say that we can't attain the perfect life before we die and go to heaven.

- Even though we may not see many examples of the perfect life in the Old Testament, isn't it still possible that there could be those under the new gift of the Holy Spirit who could live it by His power?
- Has God anywhere in the Scripture commanded us more than He promised us? Isn't it reasonable that with all the commands for us to be holy (see 1 Peter 1:15-16) that He has also provided the power to do so?

- Are the *promises* of God concerning holiness to be fulfilled in this life or only in the next? Are *all* God's promises to us (such as the promise to give us a clean heart) not meant for us until after we die?
- Is a Christian under any other laws than those which God promises to "write . . . on [our] hearts" (Jeremiah 31:31-34; Hebrews 8:10)? If God puts His law inside of us like that, what is there to keep us from living it?
- If the law is fully met in us (Romans 8:4), and we don't live according to the sinful nature but by the Spirit, how can you say that we have not been made perfect?
- Is it impossible for people in this life to "love . . . God with all [their] heart and with all [their] soul and with all [their] strength" (Deuteronomy 6:5)? Is there some other law that you are expecting Christians to fulfill that is not fulfilled by living out this love?
- Why must it take death to separate sin from us—can't the blood of Christ cleanse the soul before it leaves the body?
- Has Jesus ever taught us to pray for something that He never intended to give us? Didn't He teach us to pray, "Your will be done on earth as it is in heaven" (Matthew 6:10)? Isn't the will of God perfectly done in heaven? Then why wouldn't His will for our holiness be perfectly done here on earth?
- Why would God call us to be holy if He didn't intend to give us the power to live it?
- Didn't Paul pray according to the will of God when he prayed that the Thessalonians might be sanctified "through and through," and that they would let their "whole spirit, soul, and body, be kept blameless at the coming of the Lord Jesus" (1 Thessalonians 5:23)? Wouldn't that mean that he wanted them to be cleansed in this life and in this world? Unless he was praying for dead bodies in their graves . . . But that wouldn't make sense—why would a corpse in a coffin need to be cleansed from all sin and the desire to sin?

- Do you ever sincerely pray from the depths of your soul that God would cleanse the thoughts of your heart so you may perfectly love Him?" (Wouldn't it be foolish to pray this if you didn't think it could happen or if you really didn't want God to answer your prayer?)

I pray that God would give you the grace to consider these questions calmly and without any bias.

20 JANE'S STORY

Later that year, God called home to himself a shining light, a woman named Jane Cooper. Since she was both a living and dying witness of Christian perfection, it would be appropriate to give an account of her story, including some of her own letters, which contain the story of the manner in which God was pleased to work in her heart.

From her letters:

For as long as I can remember, I've been grateful for what God has been doing in my life. I remember hearing the minister at my church speak on Galatians 5, and I saw clearly the true state of my soul. That message described my heart and what I wanted to be—I wanted true happiness. I heard descriptions of the religion I wanted to live, I saw it like a prize in my sight, and God gave me the strength to follow closely after it. I believed God would refine me in the same way that a metal worker melts gold in the refiner's fire. Later that week, I stayed up and felt as though I would not be able to sleep unless God came and fulfilled His word to me that very night. That night I began to understand the meaning of the verse, "Be still, and know that I am God" (Psalm 46:10). I became nothing before Him and enjoyed a perfect calmness in my soul. I didn't know if God had destroyed my sin, but I wanted to find out so that I could praise Him for it. It wasn't long before doubt crept in and I was overwhelmed with unbelief. It felt like such a heavy burden and discouragement that I groaned out loud. The next day I went into the city, and there I prayed all day without stopping. I promised God that if He would save me from sin, I would praise Him for it. I was willing to give up everything so that I might have Christ. Despite my earnestness, all my prayers didn't amount to anything, and I knew that if He were to save me from sin, it was going to have to be for His own name's sake, not because of all my crying out for it. By the following day I was so depressed that I thought of killing myself or at the very least never talking to another Christian again. Even in the midst of this I still had no doubt of God's love and His ability to pardon our sins. But it was a fate worse than death to have a divided heart, to love God, but not love Him alone.

As the week went by, I sunk into deeper distress. I tried to pray, but I couldn't. I went to a friend's house, and she prayed for me, and she told me that what was happening to me was the death of my old nature, the deeply rooted sin nature within me. I returned home that night, and on the way I ran into another friend who prayed for me. Her prayer was simple, "Lord, You don't favor one person over another," and indeed, God proved that He didn't show favoritism, because He blessed my small, struggling soul. In a moment I was enabled to lay hold of Jesus Christ, and I found salvation by simple faith. God gave me the assurance that He was there in my heart, and that I would no longer struggle with evil. At that point, I worshiped Jesus and knew that He was altogether lovely, and I knew that He was mine, and all His power was at work in my life. And thanks be to God, He now reigns in my heart without rival—I have no will but His. I don't feel pride within me anymore, and my desires and affections have all taken second place to my desire for Him. I know that it is by faith that I stand, and that to keep my faith guarded I will need to keep watch and be always prayerful. But at this point in my journey, I am happy in God, and I believe He will carry me through to the next moment. I have read many times the description of love in 1 Corinthians 13 and continue to compare my heart and life against those words. When I do this, I become very aware of my shortcomings, and this makes me more aware of my need for the blood of Jesus to cover me. However, I see in myself a growing measure of the love described there, even though I am not all I shall be.

What follows here is an account of a person who was an eye and ear witness to her life. Here's what she says . . .

In the beginning of November, Jane seemed to have foresight into what was coming upon her, and she would often sing these words,

> When pain prevails over this weak flesh,
> Lamb of God pull me to your chest.

And when she wrote to me telling me that she was sick, she would write, "I am open to the will of Jesus, I give Him permission in my life—anything He sends my way is made good by His love. I am happy to think that soon Jesus will call me to come home."

When I found out that the illness she had was smallpox (at that time, this was a deadly and feared disease with no cure or immunization against it), I said to her, "Won't you be frightened if we tell you what illness you have?" She replied, "I can't be frightened because I believe that whatever comes my way is not outside of God's will for my life."

Her illness soon was very heavy upon her, but her faith was even stronger still. At one point she told me, "I have been experiencing unbelievable worship; it is as if my soul is right there in God's throne room!" Two days later I asked her if she had anything to say to me. She said only, "God is love." I asked if she had any particular promise that God had given her, and she said, "I don't desire any from Him, I am fine without seeking after anything else. I will die a lump of deformity, but when I meet you again I will be all glorious. In the meantime, the fellowship with fellow believers is a great encouragement."

By that Friday morning she said, "I believe I shall die." She then sat up in her bed and said, "Lord, I praise You that You are ever with me, and all You have is mine. Your love is greater than my weakness, greater than my helplessness, greater than my unworthiness. Lord, You say to me, this corrupted person, 'You are my sister!' and glory to You, Lord Jesus, You are my brother. Let me begin to grasp together with all the saints, how wide and long and high and deep is Your love!" Then she prayed for and blessed those standing in the room.

Some hours later, it seemed as if the agonies of death were just coming upon her, but even in the midst of it, her face was full of smiles, and she clapped her hands for joy and for victory. One of those present encouraged her, saying, "You are more than a conqueror through the blood of the Lamb." And Jane answered, "It is true, Sweet Lord Jesus. O death, where is your sting?" Then she laid down for a long time as if in a daze. When she came out of it, she tried to speak but could not. Still, she expressed her love by shaking hands with everyone in the room.

Shortly after this, our preacher arrived, and Jane was able to talk once again. The preacher asked her, "Do you believe you are saved from sin?" She told him that she did believe that and she had no doubt about it. She said that there was a time when she had doubts about it, but that was because she wasn't abiding in faith at the time. Then she declared how she had been changed saying, "I have never lived so near to the heart of Christ in my life. . . . I know now that this Christian life is not some made up story or fairy tale, for I'm happy as I can possibly be."

On Saturday morning, she prayed like this, "I know, my Lord, my life is prolonged only to do Your will. And though I may never eat or drink anything else, (she had not swallowed anything for about 28 hours), Your will be done. If it is Your will to keep me alive for four years without eating or drinking, may Your will be done—'man does not live on bread alone' (Matthew 4:4). I thank You Lord that You have taken care of those in our city who live on the streets. Our suffering is nothing compared to theirs. But I know Lord, 'that neither death nor life, neither angels nor demons, neither the present nor the future, . . . nor anything else in all creation, will be able to separate us from . . . [your] love' (Romans 8:38-39). Bless those who are in need, so that they would lack nothing. I believe He will take care of them."

On Sunday and Monday she was lightheaded, but sensible at times. It was apparent to us that her heart was still fixed on heaven. For 15 hours before she died, she was in strong convulsions: her sufferings were extreme. One person said, "You are made perfect through sufferings." She said, "More and more so." After lying quiet some time, she said, "Lord, You are strong!" Then after a long pause, she uttered her last words, "Jesus is all in all to me; glory be to Him through time and eternity." After that, she lay still for about half an hour and then died without a sigh or groan.

21 FOR THOSE WHO WANT MORE

The next year, the number of those who believed they were saved from sin continued to grow. To help them, I published an article called, "More Thoughts on the Perfect Life." Here are the main points so that we can better understand what we are talking about when we speak about "Christian perfection."

Christ: The End of the Law

1. How does this idea relate to what the Bible says about Christ being the end of the law? How is He "the end of the law so that there may be righteousness for everyone who believes" (Romans 10:4)?

Now this is going to go into some deeper theological issues, but it is important for you to understand them. There are two types of God's law referred to here. First is the law of Moses, meaning the political and moral law for God's people. Second is the law of Adam, which is the law that was given to him to live by in his innocence. You might also think of this law as the "law of good works." Under this law, people were asked to use everything that God gave them for His glory. Now realize that Adam was created to live the perfect life, without any defect. So he had no cracks or breaks in either his ability to understand what God wanted, or in his desire to do what God asked. So his "body" did not interfere with his ability to know all things clearly or to evaluate things rightly or think things through without being influenced.

So this law required that Adam should always think, speak, and act in the exact right manner in everything. He was capable of doing this, made to do this, so God was not asking him to do anything that he was unable to do.

But Adam fell, and his flawless body became flawed and corrupted. Ever since, the body has been like a stumbling block to the soul, like a ball and chain that hinders the soul from running free. So today, no person can at all times evaluate things rightly or think things through without being influenced by their broken-down desires. Since our judgment and understanding are twisted, it is impossible to make good, uninfluenced choices. Therefore, it is as easy for a person to make a mistake as it is to breathe; mistakes are now built into us, so no person is able to live up to the demands which the law of Adam requires.

However, since Christ has come, no person is required to fulfill this law. God does not require it of us anymore, for Christ is the end of the law—He fulfilled it. He completed both the law of Adam and the law of Moses. It is as if when Jesus died on the cross, the law died with Him. He has done away with both of them, and the requirement to observe either law has vanished. (So, in other words, observing these laws is no longer a condition of our salvation.)

In place of this, Christ has established a new and different law—the law of faith. The ones who receive righteousness are no longer the ones who *do*, but are now the ones who *believe*. Those who believe God and trust Christ by faith receive righteousness in the full sense of the word. That is to say, they are justified (pardoned for their sin), sanctified (cleansed from all sin), and glorified (renewed in the image of God in which they were originally made).

2. Does that make us dead to the law?

Yes! We are now dead to the law too, because of what Jesus Christ has done. He lived *the* perfect life, and fulfilled the law for us, and when He died on the Cross, the law died with Him. We are "dead to the law through the body of Christ" given for us (Romans 7:4). We are set totally free from the law by His death—because the law died with Him.

3. What does it mean then when the Bible says that we are "not free from God's law but . . . under Christ's law" (1 Corinthians 9:21)?

It means that we are no longer under the old law, but that doesn't mean that we are lawless, running wild without any law. In place of the old law, God has given us another law to live by, the law of faith. We are all under this law. We have an obligation to live in a way that reflects our relationship with the One who made us and who gave His life in exchange for ours. So God asks that we live by this new law of faith, always believing and trusting Him, and willingly doing all He asks us to do.

Love

4. Is love the fulfillment of this law?

Without question, love is the fulfillment of this law. The whole law that we are now under is completely fulfilled by being filled with God's love, and letting that love overflow out of us and into the world (Romans 13:9, 10). So, there are two things God wants from us: faith in action and a life of love. He has changed the requirements for the perfect life—He is no longer looking for "angelic perfection" where we perform as super-beings who never make mistakes, nor is He looking for us to sincerely make up for our wrongs through sacrifices. Now He wants us to love and to live our lives based completely on love. (And we can only truly love when we have been loved by the One who is love!)

5. What does it mean when the Bible says that, "love is the goal of this command" (1 Timothy 1:5)?

Love is the ultimate ending point for all that God intends. It is the target that everything in Christianity aims for. The underlying foundation is faith; we build on that and fill the whole thing with love, "which comes from a pure heart and a good conscience and a sincere faith" (1 Timothy 1:5).

6. What are the qualities and results of this love? What does it look like?

Paul reminds us that above all love is patient. It suffers through and endures all the weaknesses of the children of God and all the wickedness of the children of the world. No matter how we are injured by others, we are patient with them. Love's patience doesn't give up after a short time, but sticks with challenging people for as long as God thinks it is good to do so. Love sees the hand of God at work and willingly throws away its own agenda and joins God in what He is doing. At the same time, love is kind. In everything, it is soft, mild, tender, and gentle. Love doesn't look at others and wish to have what they have—it doesn't greedily try to keep up with the latest fashions or possessions. Love doesn't fly off the handle and act rashly or bull-headed. It doesn't jump to conclusions or put people under a microscope to judge them. It doesn't go running wild or behave offensively or indecently. It is not rude; it does not act out of character or seek its own ease, pleasure, honor, or profit. You can poke it with a stick all you want and it will not get angry, for it pushes all anger out of its heart. Love doesn't think evil thoughts or think evil of people—love gives people the benefit of the doubt and throws all jealousy, suspicion, and quick judgment into the trash. It is never happy to see other people fall into sin or wrongdoing. Instead it weeps at the sin or failure of even its most bitter enemies. Love always rejoices in the truth, holiness, and happiness of every human being. Love covers all things, speaks evil of no one, and believes all good things, especially anything that helps build another person's character. It hopes all things, to the point of looking past the obvious faults a person has, and sees them as the person they are becoming. Love endures all things—everything that God allows to come our way or that people and demons inflict upon us (1 Corinthians 13). This is the law of Christ, the law of the perfect life, the law of freedom.

This distinction between living by a law of faith (which we could call the law of love) and living by a law of works is not a small or unimportant distinction. The distinction between these is absolutely necessary to keep from being overwhelmed by thousands of doubts and fears. (If you live by works, you will always be afraid that you have not done enough . . .) It could happen to anyone, even in those who have been walking the path of love for a long time.

Stumbling?

7. But don't we all "stumble in many ways" (James 3:2), even the best of us—and even under this new law of love?

The answer is yes and no. When all our emotions, thoughts, words, and works spring from love, we are living out a purposeful life that doesn't stumble around hurting or sinning against others. But in another sense we do and will continue to trip up because we are human. In one way or another we will "stumble" as long as we remain in the body. When God fills us with love, and pours His Spirit into us, it doesn't mean that He has made us more than human and incapable of stumbling. Because our human minds are limited, and we're part of the fallen race of humanity, we can't help but make mistakes in many things. And these mistakes will frequently turn into something wrong, either in our emotions, words, or actions. For example, if we mistakenly misjudge a person's character, we may love a person less than they really deserve. And by doing that, we're led to speak or act toward that person in such a way that is not the way of love.

The Need for Christ

8. In that case, don't we need Christ on account of the fact that our mistakes may turn into something worse?

The holiest people in the world still need Christ to speak into their lives and to serve as the light of the world. Christ doesn't give us His light in some kind of bottle, so that we can take the light to guide us on our way and leave Him behind. He gives us His light moment-by-moment, so we constantly have to depend on Him. If He withdraws from us, everything turns dark. Even the holiest people in the world still need Christ as their king, to rule their lives, for God does not give any of us a stockpile of holiness. Unless we receive a *constant* supply of holiness from God, we would have nothing but unholiness left in us. We still need Christ as our priest—our link to God; our most holy stuff is not good enough, and we need Him to make everything about us beautiful and right. Even perfect holiness is only acceptable to God through Jesus Christ.

Perfect Life = Sincerity of Faith?

9. Does the perfect life mean anything more than being sincere about our faith?

If by being sincere you mean that love fills the heart, gets rid of pride, anger, desire, and self-will, rejoices evermore, praises all the time, and gives thanks in everything—then that's it—there is no more than that. But I doubt that many people use the word sincerity in this way, so I think it is best to call it what we have called it.

A person may be sincere and still have a bad attitude, pride, anger, lust, and self-will. But they're far from perfect until their heart is cleansed from these and any kind of stain or corruption.

Let me clarify this a little more: I know many people who love God with all their heart. He is their one desire, their one delight, and they're always happy in Him. They love their neighbor as they love themselves. They feel a sincere, eager, and constant desire for the happiness of every person—good or bad, friend or enemy. They are always rejoicing, praying, and giving thanks. Their souls are in continuous communication with God, in holy joy, prayer and praise. They really are living out a scriptural experience.

But even these souls dwell in a shattered body. They are so pressed down by it that they cannot always, by their own effort, act as they would like—thinking, speaking, and doing what is exactly right. Until they're no longer burdened by the fallen body of the flesh, they will keep messing up. This does not happen because of a defect in their love, but it comes from a defect in their knowledge—their fallen bodies have hindered their ability to see things exactly as they are. Even though this is the case, and in spite of that defect and its consequences, they still fulfill the law of love.

And yet they are not able to conform fully to the perfect

law. So even the most perfect people do, for this very reason, need the blood of Christ for their pardon and forgiveness. It would be right for them, (as well as others) to pray, "Forgive us our debts" (Matthew 6:12).

10. But can someone who has been saved from sin in this way be tempted?

Yes of course, just as Jesus was tempted.

Temptation vs. Corruption of the Heart

11. What you call temptation, I call corruption of the heart. How can we distinguish one from the other?

In some cases, we may not be able to distinguish one from the other without the Holy Spirit telling us which is which. But in general, we can distinguish them this way: Say someone flatters or compliments me. That is an opportunity to be tempted with pride. But instantly my soul fixes itself in a humble state before God, and I feel no pride—for I know that pride is not humility.

Say a man hits me. It is an opportunity to be tempted with anger. But my heart overflows with love, and I feel no anger at all—I'm certain that love and anger are not the same thing.

Or say someone of the opposite sex tries to entice me. Now there's an opportunity to be tempted with lust. But in an instant, I remove myself and my thoughts from that situation. In that moment I feel no desire or lust at all.

So this helps me to understand the difference. When I'm tempted, I know that it is not corruption of my heart when at that same moment my soul repels and rejects the temptation and remains filled with pure love. So temptation is something that comes from outside of me, and the corrupt heart comes from inside of me—it leads me into temptation or encourages me toward it. It becomes even easier to tell the difference between the two when I compare my present state with my past, when I was under both temptation and corruption.

Sanctification

12. But how can we know we are sanctified, saved from the heart corruption that is in us from the time we are born?

I known that I'm sanctified in the same way that I know that I'm saved and justified (made right) before God. "This is how we know that he lives in us: We know it by the Spirit he gave us" (1 John 3:24).

We know that we have been cleansed by the witness and fruit of the Spirit. First there is the witness of the Spirit. When we were first justified and made right before God, the Spirit gave affirmation and agreement with our spirit that our sins were forgiven. In the same way, when we are sanctified and cleansed, the Spirit gives us affirmation and agreement that our sins are taken away. Please remember that it is not always easy to recognize the cleansing work of sanctification at first (it is not easy to recognize that we're justified either). It doesn't always look the same after it happens, and sometimes the awareness of it is strong and sometimes it is faint. Sometimes it is completely withdrawn. But in general, the Spirit speaks to our sanctification as clearly and as steadily as He does to our salvation.

13. Isn't the cleansing of the heart self-evident in the life of the believer? Isn't the cleansing of the heart obvious?

Sometimes it is easily seen in the change in a person's actions and other times it is not. It is the same with being born again into salvation. In the hour of temptation, Satan clouds the work of God and injects all kinds of doubts and false thoughts. This is especially true in those who have either a very weak or very strong understanding of the perfect life. In times like that, we really do need God's Spirit affirming in us what God is doing and has done. Without that we would not be able to see the work of cleansing that God is doing in us. We just wouldn't be able to make it. If not for that confirmation of the Spirit, the soul could not remain in the love of God, much less continue rejoicing and giving thanks in everything. Under those circumstances, a direct witness and testimony that we are sanctified is extremely helpful.

14. Has anyone had the Spirit tell them that they will never sin?

We don't know what God might say to a particular person. However, we do not find any place in Scripture that says we cannot journey back into sin. Even those who live the perfect life (who have been cleansed from all sin) are capable of falling back into sin. (Consider this passage: "How much more severely do you think a man deserves to be punished who has trampled the Son of God under foot, who has treated as an unholy thing the blood of the covenant that sanctified him, and who has insulted the Spirit of grace?" [Hebrews 10:29]) Even those who are mature in Christ need to be reminded, "do not love the world" (1 John 2:15).

Although it may be possible that God might say to some particular person, "You will never fall into sin," we can't expect it as a rule for everyone. There's no scriptural basis for it.

Fruit of the Spirit

15. By what "fruit of the Spirit" (Galatians 5:22) may "we know that we are children of God" (1 John 5:19)?

We can know it when there is love, joy, and peace always within us. Other fruits of the Spirit include perseverance, patience, submission to God's will, gentleness, goodness, mildness, tenderness of spirit, faithfulness, simplicity, godly sincerity, meekness, calmness, evenness of spirit, steadfast character, and self-control in all things physical and spiritual.

16. But what's the big deal about having "fruits of the Spirit" as evidence? Don't we have all these fruits when we are saved?

What, are you kidding? After a sapling is first planted, does it bear fruit in a few minutes? I don't think so. When you were first saved and made right before God, could you say that you were totally surrendered to the will of God without any mixture of self-will? Did you immediately have gentleness without any touch of anger, even in the moment you were provoked? Did you possess love for your Creator and love for His creation lined up in the right priority? Did you have a proper love of self without any pride? What about love for your neighbor, with no envy, jealousy, or rash judgment? Did you have meekness to the point of an immovable calm? Self-control in everything? You can say that nobody has ever lived the perfect life if it makes you feel better, but don't say that everyone who has ever been saved automatically becomes like this the moment they become saved.

When Does Sanctification Occur?

17. But some who are newly justified and saved start into this new life right away. How do you explain that?

If they really do, then I would say that they have been sanctified, saved from sin that moment, and that they never need to lose what God has given them or feel overcome by sin anymore. Good for them!

However, that would be an exceptional case. Generally, when people are first saved, they feel in themselves some form of pride, anger, self-will, and a heart bent toward backsliding. Then God works in them to make them perfect and holy until these have gradually been put to death.

We don't need to prove over and over that there is a gradual work of God in the soul, and that He generally works over a long time (even over many years) before sin is destroyed in a person's life. But we know that God may (as a person partners with Him) cut short His work, in whatever way He pleases, and do the work of many years in a single moment. There still is a gradual work that happens both before and after that moment—so that one person may say that God's work is gradual while another may say that it's instantaneous. And the two do not contradict each other.

18. How then can those who are sealed by the Spirit "grieve the Holy Spirit of God" (Ephesians 4:30)?

Paul gives us examples to look out for. Those who have been sealed can grieve the Spirit in these ways:

- By conversations that don't build up others or offer grace,
- By falling back into bitterness or an attitude of unkindness,
- By rage, continually putting others down, or lack of tenderness,
- By anger or lack of immediate forgiveness,

- By speaking harshly, or using rough, hurtful language, and
- By speaking evil, whispering gossip, telling hurtful stories, or needlessly talking about the faults of another behind his/her back—even though it is spoken in a gentle manner.

Growing in and Falling from Grace

19. Can those who are perfect grow in grace?

Of course they can—not only while they are in the body but throughout all eternity. It may be helpful to think of Christian perfection not as a static state of "arrival," but as a dynamic life to be lived, a journey with God to be walked.

20. Can those who are perfect fall from grace?

I am convinced that they can. In the past we thought that someone who was saved from sin could not fall, but we know that is not true. We are surrounded by those who experienced perfection—they were living the perfect life—they had both the fruit of the Spirit, and the confirmation of the Spirit but have now lost both. There is no height or strength of holiness from which it is impossible to fall. The only way to keep from falling is to be completely dependent upon God and His promises of deliverance.

21. Can those who fall from this state ever return to it?

Why not? We have seen many instances of this. It is actually fairly common to go back and forth more than once before becoming established in it. Therefore, in order to guard those who are saved from sin and to keep them from every occasion of stumbling, I've written down the following advice. Just because some people stumble doesn't mean that this pursuit is impossible, or that it is not worth it. Don't give up.

Advice for Those Who Wish to Keep From Falling

22. What is the first piece of advice that you would give to guard those who are saved from sin?

Continually watch and pray against pride. If God has cast it out, don't let it come back in. It is as dangerous as any desire. We can easily slide back into it without knowing it, especially if we think that it can't happen to us. We might say to ourselves, "We attribute everything we have and do to God's glory." That may be true, but we can still be full of pride at the same time. It is pride within us that tries to give ourselves credit for everything we have and do. Pride also tries to make us think that we have things that we really do not. For example, one man gave credit to God for all of his spiritual growth, and as far as that goes, he was humble. But then he started thinking that he had grown more than any man alive, and his pride became so thick that it covered him like a cloud. If we think that God has taught us so much that we no longer need the teachings of other people—then pride is waiting at the door to pounce. We still need to be taught not only by great preachers, but also by the weakest preachers out there. God will send whomever He wants to teach us whatever we need to be taught.

There are some who have not listened to this advice, and it has led them into many prideful mistakes. Beware of the appearance of pride and of pride itself! We should have in ourselves the humble, lowly mind that Christ had. We should clothe ourselves with humility, letting it fill us on the inside and cover us on the outside. We should be modest and humble in all our words and actions, becoming the kind of people who are not out to get praise and attention for ourselves. Remember the perfect life is not about us—it is about God. And it is about God working in us to make us like His Son.

For example, we should not be so prideful that we are not willing to own up to our own mistakes and faults. If we have ever thought, said, or done something wrong, we shouldn't hesitate to acknowledge it. Don't think that if we do, it will hurt God's cause. Far from it. Be open and authentic. If anyone confronts you with something you said or did, don't evade or disguise it, but be honest about it. By doing so, you help, instead of hinder, the message of Christ.

23. What is the second piece of advice?

Beware of the offspring of pride—emotional enthusiasm,

getting carried away with excitement. If you give any place in your life to a heated imagination, you may attribute things to God that aren't from Him. Don't think that every dream, voice, impression, vision, or revelation is from God. They might be from Him. They might be from your own mind or natural random thoughts, or they might be from the devil. As the Bible says, "Do not believe every spirit, but test the spirits to see whether they are from God" (1 John 4:1). Put everything like this up against the Bible and let every insight come under its authority. You are in danger of emotional enthusiasm if you depart from Scripture even just a little. It's not smart to stray too far from the plain meaning of Bible verses or to take verses out of context. Be careful that you don't throw out human logic, knowledge, or reasoning—every one of which is a gift from God and may help your understanding of what is right. Emotions aren't bad, but getting caught up in an emotional experience that takes your focus off of God is very dangerous. Let wisdom and the Bible keep you grounded in truth, so that you don't fly away with every thought that comes into your head.

One way that people allow the imagination to carry them away is by expecting the end result without the means. For instance, some people expect knowledge without searching the Scriptures or consulting fellow believers; others expect spiritual strength without constant prayer and steady watchfulness; and still others expect blessings without hearing the Word of God at every opportunity. So they think they have received something from God without consulting the Bible or by prayer —and that is probably just their emotions. That's a dangerous place to be.

Some have ignored this attack of Satan. They stopped searching the Scriptures, saying "God writes all the Scriptures on my heart, so I have no need to read them." Others think they no longer need to hear the Word, so they stop attending church. Hear this warning if you are part of that number— that's not the wise council of God. Come back to Christ and walk the good old way, which has been given to the saints. It was written that in ancient times Christians arose early everyday to sing hymns to Christ. It is the way we stay strong as a body—we gather to worship and hear the Word.

Another starting point of this and a thousand other detours is not viewing love as the greatest gift of God. All visions, revelations, or spiritual experiences are little things compared to love—humble, gentle, patient love. All other spiritual gifts that are mentioned are less than or equal to love.

In Christianity, there is nothing higher than love. There is, in effect, nothing else. If you look for anything but more love, you are missing the point, and you have strayed from the path. So settle it in your heart right now that from the moment God saves you, you are to aim at nothing else but more of the love described in 1 Corinthians 13. You can go no higher than this until you are in God's arms in heaven.

24. What is the third piece of advice?

Watch out that you don't use your faith as an excuse to throw all God's laws out the window. Religious enthusiasm can, and does, lead to this problem. Throwing laws out the window can take a thousand different forms, so be on the lookout for any principle or practice that has any tendency to say "there is no longer any law to live by." Even the scriptural truth that "Christ is the end of the law" (Romans 10:4) may lead us into this belief—if we don't remember that He has taken every point of the former law and made it a part of the law of love. Don't fall into the trap of thinking, "Because I am filled with love, I don't need to have much holiness. Because I pray continually, I don't need to set a time for private prayer. Because I am always watchful, I don't need to examine myself." Instead we should lift up and honor all of God's law and instructions for us. Our motto should be: "Your commandments are more valuable to me than gold or gems. How I love your law! I study it all day long."

Beware of the people whose teachings throw out God's instruction or quietly push it aside. Listening to those teachings is like playing with fire. So let me encourage you in this: Don't become ingrown, caring only for those in your own close-knit church circle. Be especially careful about hanging out with only those who have experienced a spiritual renewal; this is not good. Don't turn the renewal that God has given into an exclusive club where you pat each other on the back.

Be careful that you don't get in the habit of sitting around and doing nothing with your faith. Some will tell you that you should stop doing good works—that your job now is to just sit back and soak up God's blessing. They will also say that you should not talk about your blessings because you might lose them. However, it is good to put the blessings of God into action, to do something with them, taking the blessings you have received out into the world.

25. What is the fourth piece of advice?

There is a special kind of sin that I want you to be aware of. It is called the sin of omission. Instead of being a sin of *doing* something wrong, this is a sin of *not doing something you know is right.* It is avoiding doing good. Instead, be eager to do good works. Don't willingly leave some good work undone, whether it has to do with the daily practice of the faith or some work of compassion toward others. Do all the good you possibly can to everyone you meet. In particular, "'Confront your neighbors directly so you will not be held guilty for their crimes'" (Leviticus 19:17, NLT). Don't allow your friends to walk in sin—talk to them about it. Be active. Like I said before, don't be idle, doing nothing. Be so active in God's work that no one could say that your faith is lazy or that it is only a bunch of talk. Always be about doing your job as a Christian; don't waste one moment of time. Whatever work you find to do, do it with all your might and with excellence. Watch your speech, and don't be quick to talk. "When words are many, sin is not absent, but he who holds his tongue is wise" (Proverbs 10:19). Talking too much or too long about anything is not good—it means you are probably focused on yourself and not listening to those around you. That kind of conversation is never helpful to anyone. Keep your distance from religious chitchat and gossip—don't waste time talking about holiness—live it.

26. What is the fifth piece of advice?

When we desire anything but God that is when we fall into danger. Now when you find that you desire *nothing else* but God—every other thing has been knocked out of first place in your life—make sure that the other desires and loves don't come back and try to claim the throne of your heart. Keep yourself pure. If you keep a pure focus, your whole body will be full of light. Don't allow the desire for pleasure into your life, whether it be for the taste of food or some other sense; don't be overwhelmed by the desire to please your eye or imagination. Watch that greed doesn't overwhelm you with a desire for money. And if you go around looking to be praised or puffed up by others, you are missing the point. Don't find your happiness in any creature. You don't have to fulfill any of these desires to make you happy. You are free from them, so stand in the freedom that Christ has given you!

Follow the patterns of the perfect life, which lead you to denying yourself and taking up your cross daily. We are talking about a life that is in serious pursuit of God. Take no account of any pleasure which does not bring you nearer to Him (and don't make a big deal out of any painful religious practice or sacrifice that does bring you near to Him). Simply aim at pleasing God, whether by what you do or what you must suffer through. No matter what you face, pleasure or pain, honor or dishonor, riches or poverty, let the attitude of your heart be "It's all the same to me, whether I live or die, as long as God is with me."

27. What is the sixth piece of advice?

We need to be very careful about divisions, or of doing anything that might cause a rift in Christ's Church. When churches split, it is usually because there has been a lack of unity within, and the members have stopped offering love to each other. We can't assist with any divisive attitude; it is very good not to say or do anything that would hurt the unity of the church. The first church in the city of Corinth had a problem like this because their people would compare pastors and take sides with one church leader or another. We should learn from them and realize it is not good to reject someone or run them down because they are not our favorite. And how can we make comparisons and in the process hurt someone for the sake of the cause? These are signs of consumer religion—you're "church shopping," looking for the best pastor, and your focus is all wrong. You are looking for the church to serve you rather then for you to be a minister in the church. It just leads to division. Give your leaders a break and encourage them, and don't make comparisons—it just leads to harm.

If you want to avoid a separation, split, or division in the church, don't skip meeting together. Build unity through relationships. Get into a small group for accountability, for you will find that these times of prayer, examination, and encouragement will help you in your spiritual growth and confirm in you what was preached in the service on Sunday morning. Without these connections, relationships, and spiritual support, you will struggle to grow. One hour of worship and preaching during the week is not enough.

Don't even think of separating from your brothers and sisters, whether you agree with their opinions or not. Don't think that you are so special that it is a sin if someone does not believe what you say or listen to your opinion. Your thoughts and opinions are not necessarily essential to the survival of the church. So don't be hard on those who don't see things exactly the way you see them. If someone contradicts you, so what? Relax, you'll be fine—don't cause division in the church and force people to take sides just because your feelings were hurt.

Don't give people a reason to distance themselves from you. Live well in community—more like a friendly puppy than a prickly porcupine, where people get injured just by being around you. You should practice what you preach, living out the gospel in front of people. Be especially careful when you speak about yourself. There's no need to shy away from the deep work that God is doing in your heart. Speak about it when people ask, but do it in the most inoffensive way possible. Avoid words that make you look really important. You don't need to put a label on the cleansing that God has brought you, you don't need to call it by some term like "perfection" or "sanctification" or as some have called it, "the second blessing." You don't have to make it sound like it is some higher state that you have attained. Instead, tell them the true details of the change that God brought to your life. For example, you might say, "At a certain time, I felt a change in me that is difficult to express. Since that time I have not felt pride, self-will, anger, or unbelief—nor anything but the fullness of love for God and all people." Answer any questions people ask simply and modestly. Remember the work God is doing in you is not for your glory, so that you can say you have achieved some special state. It is for God's glory.

If at anytime you fall from what you are now (if you begin to feel pride, unbelief, or the return of any attitude that you were delivered from), don't deny it or hide it or try to disguise it and live a false perfect life—doing those things would be worse for you than the fall itself. Go to someone in whom you can confide and speak just what you feel. God will enable them to speak a timely word to you, and it will strengthen you. And surely God will again lift your head; He will restore you and give you cause to rejoice in His deliverance once again.

28. What is the last piece of advice?

Be an example for others in everything, particularly in the way you live. We can say all we want that appearances aren't important, but the truth is they are. Everything about your life should be consistent with the teachings of Jesus, so that your outward life draws people to Him and doesn't push them away. Give attention to even the little things—even the clothes you wear shouldn't cause others to stumble. Watch how you spend your money. Don't throw it away on needless things but use it to make a difference because your life is making a difference. Don't live a wild, out of control life, but be solid as a rock. Let all your conversations be useful to others. In this way, you will be a light in the darkness. So live well, daily growing in grace, until the day God opens the door for you into the everlasting kingdom of our Lord Jesus Christ.

Just to reinforce all of this advice, I offer these following reflections. I hope that you will consider them deeply and thoughtfully. I would hope that you would follow these almost as closely and often as you do the Scriptures themselves!

X X X

The ocean is an excellent picture of the fullness of God and the Holy Spirit. For just as the rivers all flow back to the ocean, so the body, soul, and works of the righteous person returns to God, to live in His presence forever.

Although God is free to give out His grace at any time and in any amount that He chooses, it pleases Him to do it in connection with His people. God partners with us, and our lives and prayers matter! He blesses others through us in connection with our prayers, words of instruction, and holiness. Through these things, and through the Spirit's power, He draws souls to Him.

The depths of the soul can be completely at peace even when the person is in the midst of many outward troubles. It is just like when the bottom of the sea is calm, even while the surface is blown and tossed by a storm.

The things that help us grow in grace the most are the challenges, conflicts, and losses that come our way. We should receive them with thankfulness, preferring them to times when everything goes well. (I'm not saying that we should wish trouble on ourselves in some twisted sense, rather we should receive difficulty with thanks, realizing that God is working through it to help us grow.)

If we suffer persecution and affliction for doing right, we will be made more like Christ in that one instance than if we had just imitated His mercy by doing a bunch of good works.

Even in the midst of great difficulties and stress, it is fitting to speak of the goodness of God. Because we know nothing is out of His will and because we know He uses troubles for our good, we receive them from His hand and watch as He gives us joy in the midst of them. We are comforted to know that afflictions are part of His will and are given by Him who loves us dearly.

One way that God draws people to himself is to bring trouble, hardship, and affliction to them in the things they love the most. It makes sense, doesn't it? God gets our attention by shaking up our world and the things we had fixed our attention upon. Sometimes, He even brings trouble through good action we have done. When that happens, it clearly shows the emptiness of the things that are the loveliest and most desirable in the world.

× × ×

To be truly surrendered to God's will means that you conform your whole life to the whole will of God, Who wills and works everything that happens in this world (except sin, of course). The starting point for this kind of surrender is to embrace all the events around us, both good and bad, as part of His will. That is not to say that God wills harm upon us, but the starting place of surrender is to believe that God is working through everything. Surrender begins when we believe that He is good and loves us and will use even bad circumstances to grow us and our faith.

We should face whatever suffering may come our way with a quiet spirit. We bear our own faults and those of others by bringing them to God in secret prayer, confessing them to God in our hearts. We should not murmur or complain behind God's back for what we are going through, but instead accept that God can handle our lives in whatever way pleases Him. We are His lambs, and, therefore, ought to be ready to suffer, even to death, without complaining.

× × ×

There is no love of God without patience, and there is no patience without a lowly, humble, sweet spirit. So, if you can't be patient with those around you, don't think you have a wonderful love for God.

Humility and patience are the surest proofs that a heart has increased its ability to love.

True humility is a kind of "setting aside the self." This is the center of all other kinds of good character.

A person of humble character will listen carefully anytime they have been criticized, and they will look to see how they can improve from it.

× × ×

Carrying others through hardship and enduring any wrong done to you in meekness and silence are basic to a healthy Christian life.

God is, of course, our first love. The next most important part of the perfect Christian life is to bear the faults of others—starting with those of our own house. Love them and accept them as they are in spite of their faults.

× × ×

We have hardly ever seen God pour His Spirit out on anyone who did not pray for it at every opportunity, not just once, but many times.

God does nothing but in answer to prayer. (Even those who don't know God but start seeking Him do so because of the prayers of others.) Every victory is the result of this partnership with God in prayer.

Anytime we feel uneasy, or discouraged, we should slip away to a quiet place to pray. There we may open ourselves once again to the grace and light of God and strengthen ourselves to action, handing over to God any worry we carry about the outcome of the situations we face.

Even when facing the greatest temptation we have ever faced, a single glance to Christ and a whisper of His name are enough to overcome the evil one, so we should turn to Jesus with confidence and a calm spirit. There is no need to worry! He will be there for us.

God's command to "pray without ceasing" (1 Thessalonians 5:17, NKJV) reminds us of our desperate need of His grace to preserve the spiritual life within us. We can't live without His grace anymore than the body can live without air.

Whether we think of God or speak to Him, whether we act or suffer for Him—all is dependent upon prayer. When we have no other aim than His love and no other desire than to please Him, all of life becomes a prayerful act.

All that a Christian does, even eating and sleeping, is prayer—when it is done in simplicity and kept in its proper place among the priorities of life. If we stay in continual conversation with God all the time and don't turn some activity into something that it was not meant to be, but enjoy it as God has given it, it becomes a sacred activity, a prayerful action. Prayer continues in the heart, even when the mind is working on other things.

× × ×

It is difficult to fathom how narrow the road is where God will lead those who follow Him and how dependent upon Him we must be, lest our faithfulness fall short. We are dependent upon God for every step.

Just as a little dust can ruin a computer disk, or the smallest grain of sand can close our eyes so we can't see, so the least grain of sin that remains in our hearts will hinder its proper motion toward God.

The way we live at church should look like the way the saints are in heaven, and the way we live at home should look like the holiest of people in the church. We should do our work around the house in the same attitude that we have in prayer at church, always worshipping God from the bottom of our heart.

We should be always striving to cut off any useless things that surround us. God usually will prune back the overgrown vines of our soul in the same measure that we do our bodies—the more we cut away to produce spiritual fruit later, the more God does within us to help the process.

It is so easy to rob God of the relationship that is due Him. We may not realize that we have not included Him in our friendship or relationship with someone (even if they are a very holy person) until that relationship is taken away. If that loss produces an overwhelming, lasting sorrow, and we can't see God in the picture at that moment, then it's clear that our heart was divided and we may have put that relationship above our relationship with God. Not that we wouldn't feel sad when we lose someone, but we have to be careful that we haven't put that person ahead of God—we can't mix up our priorities—God is first in everything.

X X X

If after we have given up everything for God, we stop being watchful and don't ask God to keep watch with us, we can easily become overcome—entangled in our former ways again.

Just as dangerous winds can enter through little openings, so the devil will try to pry his way into our lives through little unobserved incidents which seem to be nothing, but can open our hearts to great temptations.

It's a good thing to renew ourselves from time to time, by closely examining the state of our souls. We need to take a fresh look at ourselves as if we were looking into our hearts for the first time. Nothing is more helpful to the full assurance of faith than examining ourselves in humility and continuing to do good.

In addition to staying watchful and prayerful, it's helpful to stay active—through school, a job, or church work. Either our old nature or our new nature will fill an empty space, and the devil tries to fill whatever we leave empty.

It's a good idea to find a partner who will pray for you and keep you accountable, but this relationship requires complete faithfulness. You should always pray for each other and help each other take a close look within—even to the point of asking about the purity of each other's thoughts and making sure your words reflect a Christian heart. You can talk together about anything, but in particular you should talk about the things of God.

× × ×

One great rule for living is this: Everyday, find out what you can do for Jesus, and do it. And since He is invisible to our eyes, we are to serve Him by serving our neighbor—which God receives as if we had served Him in person, as if He was right there visibly in front of us.

God does not want His people to be inconsistent, doing good works one day and not another. God is pleased when His people reflect His own faithfulness. Paying regular attention to our spiritual disciplines and acts of service that God entrusts to us are the marks of a faithful life.

Love fasts when it can and as much as it can. (Fasting is when you skip a meal or give up food for a day so that you can focus on prayer and being with God. It is part of the practice of denying ourselves so that we can focus on Him.) Love lives in obedience to all of God's Word and does all the good that it is capable of doing. It desires to be with God and do everything it can for God. God is so great that He turns the least thing that is done for His service into something great and wonderful.

It is better to become sick, or even lose your life for the sake of doing something good, than to live for nothing.

Do you want to do acts of love and compassion with the right attitude and motivation of the heart? Do them like this: (1) do them at the moment God gives the opportunity. (If we don't do it right at that moment, and have to come back to do something good, it appears like we are trying to make ourselves feel better, and not help the other person.); and (2) immediately afterward offer the act up to God with thanksgiving, not letting it go to our heads about how wonderful we are to be compassionate. Instead we are to be thankful for the opportunity and glad that someone was cared for. If we don't do these things, we lose the benefits of giving back to God what we have received from Him. Also, by doing this, we continue to unite ourselves to God, in prayer and in grace, and we gain strength against any bad effects that good works may produce in us. The best way to continue to be filled with the riches of grace is to pour out what we have received into good works, and not let it go to our heads. In this way, we can keep from growing tired of doing good.

Our good works themselves do not become perfect until they are lost in God—it is almost like the good works die just like we die. When they are lost in God's glory, they become something glorious themselves. This happens when they truly become something good that no longer draws attention to the act itself, or to us who may have performed the act. When good works are dead to all of that, when they have become something that God was doing in love and when they point right back to God—then they are lasting.

If we have received any favor from God, we ought to quietly get away, and take the time to say, "I have come to You Lord to restore to You what You have given, and I freely offer it up, so that I can return again to emptiness before You. For the most perfect way we can be before You is to be like an empty glass, waiting to be filled by You. The air around us is empty and capable of being filled with sunlight; it empties itself of all light at night so that it might be filled again the next day—but there is nothing in the air that tries to hold the sunlight for itself or resists being filled with it—I pray that my heart would be the same—please enable me to receive and restore Your grace and good works daily. I acknowledge that these things come from You and not from me."

22 A Summary

A few years later, I took a look back at this subject of the perfect life and wrote down the sum of what we had seen in a few short sentences:

1. There is such a thing as the perfect life. It is when God cleanses us from all sin within and makes us holy. (As part of this, He takes away even the desire to sin and replaces it with a desire to do His will; He fills us with love.) We know it is real because the Scriptures talk about the experience in many places.

2. The perfect life happens after we are saved and the guilt of our sins has been taken away (which is called justification—being pardoned and made right before God). People who have been saved are called to "go on to perfection" (Hebrews 6:1, NKJV).

3. The perfect Christian life happens in this life on earth before we die. Paul talks about those who were living but had been made perfect (Philippians 3:15, KJV).

4. The perfection we are talking about is not absolute. Absolute perfection belongs only to God, not to humans or angels.

5. Living the perfect life doesn't make any person incapable of making mistakes. Human beings aren't built that way, and we will make mistakes while we are still in these earthly, limited bodies.

6. When we say perfection, it doesn't mean "sinless perfection." That term is too tricky, so think of it this way, the perfect life is holiness, salvation from sin.

7. The perfect life is being filled with "perfect love" (1 John 4:18). This is the heart and essence of it. From this perfect love comes all of the other fruits of the perfect life—constant rejoicing, unceasing prayer, and unending thanksgiving (1 Thessalonians 5:16-24).

8. The perfect life is not an "end state," where you have arrived at a destination and have become perfect with no room for improvement. It is a journey where you can grow. In fact, someone who has been perfected in love can grow in grace far more swiftly than he or she did before.

9. Because we are dealing with human beings, this condition of holiness which we live in can be lost if we don't continue in it. We have seen this happen many times. It can be lost, but don't forget that it can be restored as well.

10. The perfect life is surrounded by a gradual, step-by-step work of God in our lives. Before we see the leaps and bounds of growth in the perfect life, God has been working, and He continues to work in us after we receive it.

11. Does Christian perfection itself happen all at once or not? To look at this, let's break it down:
    - It seems to happen all at once in some believers.
    - After that change, we see them enjoying perfect love—they feel the fullness of love, and only love, and they are full of continual joy, prayer, and thanksgiving. This is all that I am talking about when I say perfection, so those that have had this experience are good examples of what I am talking about.
    - "But in some people, the change did not happen all at once." For these it is possible that they did not notice the instance when it happened. (Think of it like this: It is often difficult to tell the exact moment a

person dies, yet there is an instance that their life ceases. It is important to remember that if sin is ever ended in us, there must be a final moment of its life in us and a first moment of our deliverance from it.)

- "But if they have this love now, they will lose it." They might, but they don't have to. And whether they lose it or not, they have it now! They now experience the perfect life that we are talking about. They are now all love, they now rejoice, pray, and praise God continually.

- "But this teaching of this perfect life has been abused, misunderstood, and twisted around." So have many other teachings, including what it means to be saved. That is no reason to give up on this or any other scriptural idea. Don't throw the baby out with the bath water.

- "But those who think they are saved from sin say that they have no need for what Christ has done." Actually, they say the opposite. Their language is, "Every moment, Lord, I want the benefits of Your death applied to me!" When this work of God happens to them, they have a deeper conviction of their need for Christ and all that He offers them than they have ever had before.

- Therefore, all our leaders should make a point of preaching and teaching about the perfect life to all believers, constantly encouraging them to pursue it, talking about it plainly and strongly. All believers should listen to what they say and pursue the perfect life with everything that is within them.

23 A Plea for Understanding

I have done what I have set out to do. I have given a plain and simple account of what we have seen God doing in our midst and described it as best I can. I have talked about the perfect life in the way that I received it and have seen it. I have tried to paint a picture of it, without disguising it or covering anything up.

And I would ask anyone (who hasn't closed off their mind), what are you afraid of? Why does the idea that God can make us holy seem so strange that Christians would react like the world is coming to an end and all religion has been torn up by the roots when they hear of it? Why is it that Christians can't bring themselves to mention "perfection" or talk at all about how God can enable us to live a perfect life? Is there any reason to plug our ears when a preacher speaks about it? I believe there is no good reason. Yet there are some who oppose the idea strongly. They looked for something to hold against me, and this is what they found, "He preaches his own idea of perfection!" Well, I do preach perfection, but it is not my own idea. The idea comes from Jesus Christ. It is His idea alone. These are the words of Jesus, not mine, "Be perfect, therefore, as your heavenly Father is perfect" (Matthew 5:48). And who is going to say against Him that we can't be?

This idea was picked up by the apostles—Paul, James, Peter, and John—it is not just my idea. It is the doctrine of everyone who teaches the whole truth of the gospel. Do you want to know where I found this idea of the perfect life? I found it in the Bible, in the Old and New Testaments, when I was reading them with no other purpose than the salvation of my own soul. But no matter where you think it comes from, I ask you, what harm is there in pursuing a holy, perfect life?

Take another look at it from every angle. In one view it is purity of intention, the dedicating of life to God. It is giving God all of our heart; it is one desire and design ruling all our attitudes, emotions, and character. It is devoting to God, not just a part, but all our soul, body, and substance. Looking at it from another view, it is having the mind of Christ, which enables us to walk as He walked. It is the sacrificial devotion to a permanent covenant with God, cutting away all filthiness—all inner and outer pollution. It is a renewal of the heart in the full image of God, conforming us once again to the full likeness of our Creator. In another view, it is loving God with all our heart and loving our neighbor as ourselves. So, take it in any view you please, (there is no real difference), for this is the whole and complete definition of the perfect life and of Christian perfection. This is what all my writings point toward, and what I have taught all my life.

24 A FINAL DEFENSE

Now if you take this perfection in its true form, who can speak against it? Will anyone dare say that it is a bad idea to love God with all our heart and love our neighbor as ourselves? Who will say a word against the renewal of the heart, not just in part, but completely in the whole image of God? Who will open their mouth against being cleansed from all pollution of both flesh and spirit or against having the mind of Christ and walking as Jesus walked? What people who call themselves Christians are able to object to the devotion of not just part, but all of their soul, body, and substance to God? What serious believers would oppose giving God all of their heart and having their desire for Him control every attitude? Let me say again, if you allow this perfect life to appear in its own shape, not some twisted version or made-up idea of it, who can fight against it? You would have to disguise it or change it before you opposed it. You would have to first dress it up in a lion's fur, and put teeth and claws on it before any normal "gazelle" of a Christian could be made to worry about it.

Whatever you do, don't let the children of God fight any longer against becoming like Jesus—or being renewed in the image of God. Don't allow the members of the body of Christ to say anything against having the mind that was in Christ. Don't let those who are alive in God oppose the complete dedication of our lives to Him. Why would those who have His love poured into their hearts resist giving all their hearts to Him? Doesn't everything within you cry, "How can we who have been loved, love enough?" It would be a shame for those who desire to please Him to be filled with any other desire but to love fully.

Why should these religious people, these devout Christians, be afraid of complete devotion? Why should those who love Christ count it a fatal mistake to think that they could have all the mind of Christ?

We are saying that we are made right before God freely through the righteousness and the blood of Christ. And why do people oppose us for expecting that we will also be made wholly clean from sin through His Spirit? We don't expect those who serve sin, or those who are only going through the motions of religion, to agree with us. But how long will those who worship God in spirit, who have made a covenant to follow God, stand against those who seek to have all sin cut away from their lives, and who thirst to be cleansed from "all filthiness of the flesh and spirit perfecting holiness in the fear of God" (2 Corinthians 7:1, NKJV)?

Are we enemies with the church because we look for a full deliverance from "the sinful mind [which] is hostile to God" (Romans 8:7)? No, we are your brothers and sisters, your co-workers in the vineyard of the Lord, your companions in the kingdom of Jesus. Stand with us, even though we make this confession (whether it is foolishness or not): we do expect to love God with all our heart and our neighbor as ourselves. Yes, we do believe that God will, in this world, cleanse the thoughts of our hearts by the power of His Holy Spirit, and that we shall perfectly love Him, and worthily lift up His holy name.

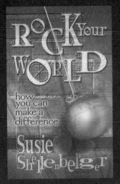